MAKERSPACES
IN SCHOOL

A Month-by-Month Schoolwide Model for
Building Meaningful Makerspaces

MAKERSPACES
IN SCHOOL

A Month-by-Month Schoolwide Model for
Building Meaningful Makerspaces

Lacy Brejcha

PRUFROCK PRESS INC.
WACO, TEXAS

Library of Congress Cataloging-in-Publication Data

Names: Brejcha, Lacy, 1980- author.
Title: Makerspaces in school : a month-by-month schoolwide model for building
  meaningful makerspaces / Lacy Brejcha.
Description: Waco, TX : Prufrock Press, Inc., [2018] | Includes
  bibliographical references.
Identifiers: LCCN 2018018581 (print) | LCCN 2018029061 (ebook) | ISBN
  9781618217813 (eBook) | ISBN 9781618217820 (ePub) | ISBN 9781618217806
  (pbk.)
Subjects: LCSH: Maker movement in education. | Makerspaces.
Classification: LCC LB1029.M35 (ebook) | LCC LB1029.M35 .B74 2018 (print) |
  DDC 371.39--dc23
LC record available at https://lccn.loc.gov/2018018581

Edited by Katy McDowall

Cover and layout design by Allegra Denbo

ISBN-13: 978-1-61821-780-6

Printed in the United States of America.

At the time of this book's publication, all facts and figures cited are the most current available. All telephone numbers, addresses, and website URLs are accurate and active. All publications, organizations, websites, and other resources exist as described in the book, and all have been verified. The author and Prufrock Press Inc. make no warranty or guarantee concerning the information and materials given out by organizations or content found at websites, and we are not responsible for any changes that occur after this book's publication. If you find an error, please contact Prufrock Press Inc.

Prufrock Press Inc.
P.O. Box 8813
Waco, TX 76714-8813
Phone: (800) 998-2208
Fax: (800) 240-0333
http://www.prufrock.com

Dedication

To Jim, my husband, I'm so grateful you're the person I get to do life with. You support me and cheer me on, and are patient when my passions aren't always convenient. You truly love me unconditionally . . . that must be hard!

To Brooke, my oldest daughter, you're sporty yet refined, are relentlessly creative in ways that are uniquely your own, are observant, and have a great moral compass.

To Grace, my youngest daughter, you're fashionable in your own unique way, carefree, spirited in a way that I hope you never lose, and my sweet snuggle buddy.

I love you three with every ounce of my being. Remember, God is the source of your confidence and self-worth. You are fearfully and wonderfully made—be you!

To my mom, who always told me to pursue my dreams, no matter what they were or how odd they may have been, I love you and thank you!

To all kids . . . especially those who learn differently and have to work extra hard at school in the regular classroom setting. You are the reason I'm passionate about the maker mentality because you are successful in making and this is where you shine. Don't miss out on opportunities that could be great just because they may also be extremely challenging.

Table of Contents

Foreword...ix

Introduction 1

Chapter 1   August
             What Is a Makerspace? 3

Chapter 2   September
             Why Are Makerspaces Important? 23

Chapter 3   October
             Makerspace Planning and Wonder Walls 41

Chapter 4   November
             Developing and Implementing Makerspace Activities .. 55

Chapter 5   December
             Providing Assessment and Recording Standards 75

Chapter 6   January
             Being Resourceful: Requesting Donations for
             Materials, Getting Helpers or Outside Experts, and
             Help . . . We Don't Have Room for a Makerspace! 93

Chapter 7   February
             Keeping a Makerspace Planned, Playful, and Purposeful.. 105

Chapter 8   March
             Structured Versus Unstructured Makerspaces in a
             Classroom, Schoolwide, or Districtwide Model 121

Chapter 9   April
             The Problem-Solving Process and
             Presentations of Projects and Challenges 137

Chapter 10   May
             Technology Integration and High(er) Tech Materials .. 149

Conclusion: Keep Making 169

References 171

Appendix: Additional Resources 175

About the Author.. 179

Foreword

A schoolwide Makerspace program offers students a place to create, collaborate, and grow. Three years ago we had a vision to create more opportunities for students to direct their own learning and think outside the box. Over the last 3 years, the Makerspace time has become one of the favorite parts of the students' days. Their weekly classes consist of teacher challenges that allow students to take ownership in their learning, nurture creativity, and problem solve. We have seen that the students have grown in their abilities to problem solve, evaluate, and engage in productive debates. It has allowed students a safe place to fail. Students are learning that failing at something and having to reevaluate and reconstruct are parts of the learning process. They are consistently trying to make things better rather than being satisfied with just having a project "done."

—Kelly Bray
Elementary Principal, Bosqueville ISD

Introduction

> My best teachers were not the ones who knew all
> the answers, but those who were deeply excited by
> questions they couldn't answer.
>
> —Brian Greene

Through Makerspaces, project-based learning provides opportunities for credible, legitimate, and authentic growth and development. This book will allow any educator to walk away with a plan to create a Makerspace in his or her classroom or a school- or districtwide model that works for many. Makerspaces are very fluid places—each is unique in its own way!

This book is organized by months to help you ease into creating a Makerspace. For organization purposes, we will start in August for Chapter 1. "Targets" are given for each month as well as "Planning Pages and Reflections," so you can record your thoughts and start planning about what you have learned and want to implement. Target goals are reviewed at the end of each chapter in these planning pages.

The goal is for you to start easy and ease into creating *your* Makerspace. This should be a fun journey. In August and September, you'll get your bearings and define what a Makerspace is to you and why it will be beneficial for *your* students. You'll also explore research about the importance of STEAM (science, technology, engineering, art, and math) education, and be introduced to a problem-solving process that will guide you and your students through each Makerspace challenge or activity. By October, you will be implementing your Wonder Wall and begin to have a good grasp on how your Makerspace will look and be managed. By November, you will be implementing some simple, yet planned, purposeful, and playful activities into your Makerspace. If you are not starting in August, no problem. Just start with Chapter 1 and take it one chapter/month at a time. I know you are busy and overwhelmed with all of the other aspects of teaching. I have been very intentional in making sure you can accomplish every target, reflection, and activity given in each chapter within the month. If you feel like moving more quickly through the chapters, that's great, too.

CHAPTER 1: AUGUST

What Is a Makerspace?

[A] space where kids have the opportunity to make—a place where some tools, materials, and enough expertise can get them started. These places, called makerspaces, share some aspects of the shop class, home economics class, the art studio, and science labs. In effect, a makerspace is a physical mash-up of different places that allows makers and projects to integrate these different kinds of skills.

—Dale Dougherty, *Design, Make, Play*, 2013

TARGETS FOR AUGUST

* Define what a Makerspace is and what the word means to you, your campus, administration, and/or any other stakeholders. No two Makerspaces are the same.
* Brainstorm ways your Makerspace can help you cover state and local mandated standards.

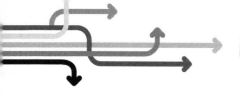

You might be thinking, "What in the world is a Makerspace? What does this word even mean? Will this 'space' even help me cover state/locally mandated standards?" Creating a Makerspace can be extremely intimidating. I have done it—and it can be scary. In general, Makerspaces and making are subjects that people do not know a lot about or have not experienced before. But we can do this. We have to do this for our students. We have to change the way we provide enrichment and innovation to prepare our students for more. Our students will be competing for jobs that don't even exist yet, and we have to prepare them to be ready for this challenge.

Makerspaces bring joy back to learning. Anticipate and plan for students to be excited and actively engaged in your Makerspace. Get ready to move students from passive learners to active learners, and prepare to become a facilitator of learning yourself. Students will love Makerspace time. In fact, it might very well be the reason a student likes school on the days he or she gets to visit your Makerspace. I have had many parents tell me that on their child's Makerspace day, he or she is happier to come to school and has a better attitude in the morning overall.

I have written this book in a reflective way to create a guide of what I wish I had known before and as I began implementing a Makerspace. Hopefully, you can learn from my successes and failures—I have certainly had both!

Makerspaces bring joy back to learning. Anticipate and plan for students to be excited and actively engaged in your Makerspace. Get ready to move students from passive learners to active learners, and prepare to become a facilitator of learning yourself.

In general terms, a Makerspace is a place and time for students to create, tinker, learn how to do something new, be challenged, have fun, explore, problem solve, imagine, build, draw, write, make, work with their hands, think critically, be persistent, make real-world connections, and use technology. It is a very fluid space, and no two are exactly alike. If your students are making, you have a Makerspace. This type of learning supports the 21st century and—most importantly—*beyond*.

Bringing a Makerspace to your school will:
* allow students to be creative thinkers and makers,
* allow students to recognize that failures can lead to success if they are persistent,
* create excitement for learning,
* allow students to make products that all look different (not a cookie-cutter approach),
* allow students to collaborate and learn from each other,
* create ways for students to ask real questions that involve the real world,
* encourage students to pursue passions and wonders,
* create problem solvers,
* create endurance and grit in students to complete projects,
* expose students to materials they may have never used before, and
* encourage students to reflect as they use a problem-solving process.

This book will be very real and feasible, and the activities described are obtainable and realistic. I intend to be *very real* with you. So often as educators we sit through a workshop or training and come away with nothing that is actually practical to implement in our classrooms. This is not that type of book. My biggest annoyance in education is when my time is wasted—it's so frustrating. With so much to do already, I need practical ideas and inspiration. As I write this book, I am "in the trenches," working with students day in and day out. I get you; I am you! I go home *so tired*, just like you at the end of every day, but I know I am making a difference, as are you.

I am currently in my 16th year as a public school teacher. I graduated from Baylor University in 2002 and went directly into teaching. I currently run the Makerspace program for 300+ students in grades K–5. I also am the gifted and talented teacher at the elementary level and the district GT coordinator and instructional technologist on campus. I am blessed with two amazing and highly inquisitive daughters, Brooke and Grace, and a very supportive and loving husband, Jim. My kids are still young and still have a lot of schooling to complete. I want them to be challenged, creative, innovative, and savvy with a variety of technology, and become expert problem solvers. I also have many wonderful coworkers, friends, and great administra-

tors who listen and provide feedback as well. For that, I am forever grateful.

Q: What are some big takeaways (skills, mindsets, relationships) you've seen your students leave Makerspace with?

A: Students who struggle in regular classrooms thrive in Makerspace, and their self-esteem increases greatly. They realize they *can* do it . . . kids learn by doing that persistence pays off!

For the Makerspace program, I see all students in grades 1–5 once a week for 45 minutes. On their Makerspace day, students do not go to PE. Kindergarten comes every other week for 30 minutes. Students love Makerspace and look forward to coming. Before I took my current position, I will admit that I knew I needed more, and the students needed more. In my heart, I knew education was my calling and my passion, but I was reaching a point in my career when I was beginning to feel burnt out. But now I know: We can change education and make it better. We can make it more innovative, creative, and fun.

Getting Started

> We ask children to do for most of a day what few
> adults are able to do for even an hour. How many
> of us, attending, say, a lecture that doesn't interest
> us, can keep our minds from wandering? Hardly any.
> —John Holt, *How Children Fail*, 1995

As you begin to conceptualize your Makerspace in these first few chapters, I will provide you with field-tested and research-based knowledge that shows how Makerspaces can serve students (high, low, and middle achieving) and teachers alike. For example, according to one estimate, 65% of today's students will one day be employed in jobs that have yet to be created (as cited in World Economic Forum, 2016). Thus, we must teach our students to be creative inventors, entrepreneurs, and future productive employees. They must possess required trade skills and soft skills.

So many (read: most) of our students are bored every day at some point. That does not mean that, as educators, we are doing a poor job. I honestly believe that the vast majority of educators are doing the best they can. We have so much to teach and cover, so many students to account for, and so much to do, including writing lesson plans, accounting for students with special needs or those who require advanced content, developing Individuated Education Plans (IEPs) and behavior intervention plans (BIPs), and caring for students who come to school hungry or need someone to brush their hair or provide them with a toothbrush and toothpaste, etc. We are not just educators. We are advocates for kids, and you are just what your students need. Keep going, please! Our students urgently need *you*. You are enough, and you have what it takes to help your students start making. Rather than teaching the curriculum, teach your students, and the curriculum will follow. But as you begin to build your Makerspace, don't be afraid to fail. A Makerspace will require you to (1) take risks and (2) be prepared to regroup and switch gears when necessary.

Risk-Taking

If you are reading this book, it tells me you are looking for ways to provide your students with trial-and-error, constructive, experimental, and collaborative learning through hands-on activities. If you are not a little (or extremely) uncomfortable each year that you teach, you are not growing personally and trying new things. Risk-taking requires us to be extremely vulnerable and be willing to fail. You will fail some days, and you will soar many days. Let's agree right here that this is to be expected. It is okay. Just like I tell my students, "If you fail, if it doesn't work, if you get frustrated . . . it is okay! Keep trying; you've got this." If you are reading this as required reading material or are unsure if a Makerspace is right for you, I encourage you to have an open mind. I know that your days will be more fun and fulfilling if you implement the ideas presented in this book. Hang in there with me.

You and I don't have to have it all figured out; we just have to keep moving forward and trying until we get it right. We can make educa-

Our students urgently need *you*. You are enough, and you have what it takes to help your students start making.

tion fun. Are any parents excited to see their child's folder stuffed full of papers? What about when he or she brings home something he or she made, invented, created . . . and actually wants to talk about? Let's make that our goal. I hear many students reference projects we have done before and ask if we can do them again because they have a new idea or a better plan of execution. This tells me that although they have likely forgotten what was covered on a worksheet, they have not forgotten what challenge, creation, or project that they did or made in our Makerspace. Even better, they are reflecting during their time outside the classroom on making a prototype better or redesigning a project for better results. These are kids who will be employable and a joy to work with in the real world.

Regrouping and Switching Gears

Since I graduated with my degree in education, I have taught in the elementary classroom setting in a variety of grade levels, ranging from Pre-K to grade 5. Although I felt very prepared in many ways after graduation, there is much learning that cannot take place until you are in the trenches day in and day out with our most precious resources—our students. If I were asked to develop one course to add to an education degree, it would be "How to Regroup and Switch Gears . . . in 5 Minutes or Less."

We can plan what we think is an amazing lesson, and as we begin teaching it or trying it, we quickly see it is not working. Regroup, switch gears, and *keep going*. I always like to have a Plan B. Almost 90% of the time you won't need it. The 10% you do, you will be thrilled you were prepared. This is especially true when using technology. I am the instructional technologist on our campus, so I should be able to figure out a technical difficulty fairly quickly. Not always so! Last year during my big evaluation, where I was using a ton of technology, the Wi-Fi went down. Not good . . . but there was also nothing I could do about it right then. It happens . . . regroup, switch gears, and keep going! This is an area I see many educators struggle with. They have a hard time accepting that what was supposed to happen is not working. Undoubtedly, some of this pressure is created by unsupportive colleges and administrators who expect to see you doing exactly what is in your lesson plan. The truth is, the best learning happens when we loosen the reins a little and let the learning unfold on its own. This is part of a plea to administration and stakeholders in districts to reevaluate their thoughts in this area. Rather than checking to see that what is happening in the classroom is exactly what is on the lesson plans, listen to the language you hear kids using as they work on problems and solve challenges. Look for the learning that is going on. Typically with great teachers, what you hear and see is 100% better than what the lesson plans state. Be open-minded.

Developing a Unique STEAM-Based Makerspace

My hope is that you will walk away with a plan to implement a Makerspace in your classroom or a school/district model that works for your unique situation. No two are the same, and the way a Makerspace operates and looks varies greatly depending on what skill is being covered during a particular week or unit. Makerspaces are very fluid places—just go with it. Remember, if something doesn't work, then regroup and try again. What your space looks like will vary greatly compared to others, but what your students are doing is the same. Your students should be:

- thinking,
- trying,
- problem solving,
- questioning,
- testing,
- failing in a safe environment,
- reflecting and redesigning,
- planning,
- learning,
- creating,
- using teamwork,
- inventing, and
- collaborating with peers.

Makerspaces provide authentic, hands-on learning when modeled around STEAM (science, technology, engineering, art, and math).

A schoolwide model can successfully be created using my problem-solving process (discussed in the next section) and other tips and tricks shared throughout this book. In a Makerspace, all students are serviced. Makerspaces are environments where special education, regular education, and gifted students can all have their needs meet. As well as allowing for differentiation, Makerspaces build students' job skills, expose students to new ideas, cultivate soft skills, and engage students in their learning.

Building Job Skills

Although STEAM career paths have made huge gains over the past 15 years, the way we educate children has not. Read that sentence again. This is so strange to me. STEAM jobs are not being filled at the rate that they are being created or needed, and we must begin addressing this as early as elementary school. The World Economic Forum (2016) produced a report that predicted what the employment landscape will look like in 2020 based on responses from chief human resources and strategy officers from leading global employers. Figure 1 outlines skills that will be sought by employers in 2020, compared to the skills sought in 2015.

STEAM jobs are not being filled at the rate they are being created.

As a nation, our education industry has recognized a shortcoming in our students. We've fallen behind other industrialized countries in terms of STEM-related fields (Kroeger, 2016), which include science, technology, engineering, and math. I prefer a STEAM approach, adding art as part of the Makerspace model. This type of focused education opens students to explore new topics and subjects, and it also allows for different learning techniques to be promoted. Creativity in Makerspace promotes innovative thinking in students. When you put your focus on project-based learning and problem solving, which are absolutely required in a Makerspace modeled around STEAM, you provide opportunities for credible, lifetime, and authentic growth and development.

Top 10 Skills Employers Are Likely to Seek in 2020	Top 10 Skills Sought by Employers in 2015
1. Complex problem solving	1. Complex problem solving
2. Critical thinking	2. Coordinating with others
3. Creativity	3. People management
4. People management	4. Critical thinking
5. Coordinating with others	5. Negotiation
6. **Emotional intelligence**	6. Quality control*
7. Judgment and decision-making	7. Service orientation
8. Service orientation	8. Judgment and decision-making
9. Negotiation	9. Active listening*
10. **Cognitive flexibility**	10. Creativity

FIGURE 1. Skills sought by employers. Adapted from World Economic Forum (2016). (*Note. Skills emphasized in bold are new to 2020, and skills marked with asterisks [*] no longer appear in the Top 10 in 2020.*)

Mike Rowe, the television host known for his work on the Discovery Channel series *Dirty Jobs*, has made numerous videos and given many podcasts that remind us that technical jobs are profound and that a 4-year degree is not the best path for all. According to Rowe, if trade workers stopped going to work, they would effectively bring the economy to its knees (as cited in ATTN, 2017). We need a variety of employable adults with skill sets necessary for the jobs that they will fill. Makerspaces are great places to introduce students to these types of skills.

Perhaps one of the most rewarding aspects of having the privilege to teach a Makerspace is that I get to see students excel in my classroom who typically aren't great in other areas of school academics. To see them feel successful and find something they love is the absolute best. You will be so surprised at what students are good at. I have one student, in particular, who struggles with typical classroom assignments but thrives in our Makerspace. If I have a broken piece of furniture or a broken piece of equipment, I save it for him to fix. He loves this and is a mastermind at fixing items without needing much help, if any, from me. It's his thing, and he shines! He will excel in the job force because of this trait.

When students are armed with potential career paths and interests and feel successful, it affects every other aspect of their day.

Students love Makerspace and don't want to miss it. Because of this, parents are curious about what Makerspace is, so be sure to communicate with them about happenings in your class and ways they can be involved. I further discuss talking to parents about Makerspaces in Chapter 6.

The Importance of Exposure

Oftentimes, students don't really know what they like because they have not had exposure or had the opportunity to try new things out. This is where a Makerspace can come in. This year while using littleBits electrical circuits, I had a female student tell me, "I'm not an electrical type of girl." By the end of class, however, she had an electrical circuit that made noise, had blinking lights, and made a fan blow. Needless to say, she is now an electrical type of girl! The items we provide students access to may not necessarily seem awesome to us, but many of your students may not have access at home to simple things like LEGOs, K'Nex, or magnetic blocks, to name only a few tools. The students who do have access to these items will discover them in a whole new light when they are given a challenge or problem to solve using these items. Don't underestimate the power of something that seems simple.

Cultivating Soft Skills

Our students must also have "soft skills" to succeed in the 21st century. Soft skills are personal attributes that enable someone to interact effectively and harmoniously with other people (Wikipedia, 2018). A combination of interpersonal people skills, social skills, communication skills, character traits, attitudes, career attributes, and emotional intelligence (see Figure 1), soft skills enable people to effectively navigate their environment, work well with others, perform well, and achieve their goals with complementing hard skills. The Collins English Dictionary defines "soft skills" as "desirable qualities for certain forms of employment that do not depend on acquired knowledge: they include common sense, the ability to deal with people, and a *positive flexible attitude*." Makerspaces lend themselves well to the development of soft skills as well as science, technology, engineering, arts, and math skills. A Makerspace is a win-win when it comes to teaching any of these skills.

Differentiation

Makerspaces naturally lead to differentiation when planned appropriately. Students who have varied learning needs thrive in a Makerspace. This is because of the nature of a Makerspace in general. STEAM-related activities can prepare *all* of our students to actively seek and enjoy science, technology, engineering, art, and math. For example, my special needs, gifted, and regular education students all come to Makerspace with their homerooms. I have appropriate activities planned for our special needs students if modification is needed, such as during LEGO or K'Nex challenges (see Chapter 4). You could provide larger LEGOs for students still working on developing fine motor skills or for students who put items in their mouths. The same principle applies to K'Nex pieces and other materials. Younger students or special needs students can work on the same skills as older students or peers just by changing up the size of the manipulatives. Your goal is the process, not the product. Let each child work at his her own pace through problem solving. What matters is the process, not the product.

STEAM-related activities can prepare *all* of our students to actively seek and enjoy science, technology, engineering, art, and math.

Through differentiation in Makerspaces:
- Students can express themselves without fear of failure.
- Materials, supplies, and challenges are adaptable to all learners.
- By properly planning your Makerspace, you can build an environment that encourages the process over the product. Encourage tinkering, play, and open-ended challenges and concepts.
- Regardless of students' academic level and/or English language proficiency, they can begin making with very little

teacher facilitation of learning. Makerspaces offer flexible, self-directed learning environments.

- By using the problem-solving process (described in the following section), students can work at a pace that works for them, and teachers can easily see where each student is at in the process.
- Materials, activities, and supplies are provided to meet the needs of mixed-ability learners.
- While collaborating with their peers, students of varying abilities work together, creating a culture of making.

More than that, Makerspaces force students to leave their comfort zones and are challenging, fun, busy, messy, loud . . . basically controlled chaos! But don't let that deter you.

Student Engagement

What stands out the most to me is that students are highly engaged and focused on what they are doing. Behavior is rarely a problem because students are so engaged. They question each other, question themselves, solve problems, and create. These are all high-level thinking skills that keep the brain engaged. Often times, an adult will come into my classroom and no students will even notice! They are so focused on and consumed with making and learning that outside stimuli go unnoticed. My principal noticed this when she came in to observe. After she had been in our Makerspace for 15 minutes or so, a student looked up at her and asked her when she had gotten into our room.

Introducing a Makerspace
Problem-Solving Process

Through my problem-solving process, students define problems, plan solutions, make a model or plan a strategy, test the model, and always reflect and redesign as needed. These five steps help bring focus and structure to a very busy environment. I will introduce my problem-solving model in this section and in more detail in the chapters that follow, but I love this process because during a challenge, groups work at their own pace. As I facilitate, I always ask, "Where are you in our problem-solving process?" This brings focus, structure, and mindfulness as students work. Students are responsible for their own learning and for completing the task at hand. The process helps to define clear guidelines and bring purpose to the challenge at hand.

Problem-Solving Process Poster

The problem-solving process poster (see Figure 2) outlines the five steps:
1. Define the problem or challenge.
2. Plan solutions.
3. Make a model or plan a strategy.
4. Test the model or try it out.
5. Reflect and redesign.

A color-coded version of the poster is available on the book's webpage (https://www.prufrock.com/makerspaces-in-school-resources.aspx). For your youngest learners or special needs students, you may prefer to provide a poster like Figure 3 (also available in color on the book's webpage).

This problem-solving process not only works for challenges related to Makerspace but even behavior. I had a colleague who used this for discipline. Take, for example, a child who destroys or vandalizes school property. First you have him or her define the problem (e.g., I got angry and broke the keyboard by smashing it with my fist). Next, he or she plans solutions (e.g., I can try to fix the keyboard; I can buy a new one). Remember, the student must come up with these answers. That is part of the process. After that, he or she needs to plan a strategy (e.g., How can I earn money to buy a new keyboard?). Next, he or she tries out the strategy (e.g., after buying a new keyboard, he or she hooks it up to be certain it is working). Lastly, he or she reflects (e.g., writing down what he or she learned, most likely that it was a huge pain to fix what he or she did).

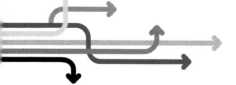

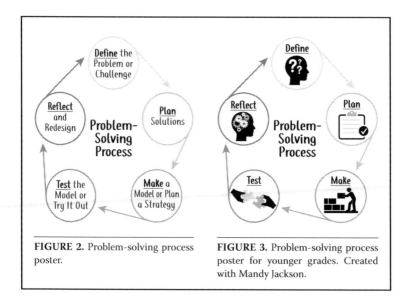

FIGURE 2. Problem-solving process poster.

FIGURE 3. Problem-solving process poster for younger grades. Created with Mandy Jackson.

Meeting State and Federally Mandated Standards

State and federally mandated standards are easy to weave into the context of a Makerspace. We will discuss my problem-solving process more in later chapters, but you can see by looking at this process, many standards are easily weaved into the day-to-day context of a Makerspace. On our campus, each classroom has a problem-solving poster on display. Some very general examples of how mandated standards are met in a Makerspace are included in Table 1. For each area of STEAM, I will go into more detail on how standards are covered in the following chapters.

Just Start Making

Don't be deterred by the fact that you don't yet have a space or a room solely dedicated to your Makerspace. You can start right now by creating a cart or tub of supplies for your own classroom or one that teachers can check out for use in their classrooms. A fun name, such as "Engineering Cart," gets students excited. At first, you can provide simple materials, such as LEGOS or K'Nex, along with challenges for

Table 1

How Makerspaces Meet Standards

General Standard	How It Looks in Makerspace (Referenced Back to Problem-Solving Process Poster by Color)
Obtaining, Evaluating, and Communicating Information	Documenting and sharing during the design process. (Entire Process)
Constructing Explanations and Designing Solutions	Using data and drawing conclusions to plan solutions. (Yellow and Red)
Analyzing and Interpreting Data	Use a variety of formats to plan solutions. (Red)
Developing and Using Models	Activities and the problem-solving process require making a model or planning a strategy. (Purple)
Asking Questions and Defining Problems	Begin by defining the problem and planning solutions by asking questions and brainstorming. (Yellow and Red)
Designing Solutions	Problem-solving process. (Red)
Teamwork (Soft Skill)	Students must work together to share space and materials. (Purple, Blue, and Green)
Learning Strategies	Makerspaces are student-driven, so students are naturally drawn to activities that facilitate their learning styles.
Goal-Setting	(Entire Process)
Design a Product or Project	(Entire Process)
Flexibility	Rework possible solutions until a solution is reached. (Green)
Perseverance	(Entire Process)
Taking Risks	Making is risk-taking at its finest. There is no guarantee what you do will work.
Opinions and Sources of Information	Making requires gathering information and deciding if it is important and relevant.
Application of Prior Knowledge	While planning solutions, making models, and testing models, student continually draw from their prior knowledge relating to the task at hand. (Red, Purple, Blue, and Green)
Problem Solve	(Entire Process)
Technology	Students use a VAST amount of technology, including coding and so much more. Examples are given throughout the book and specifically in Chapter 10.
Digital Citizenship	Sharing learning through a variety of digital platforms, using the internet wisely, and researching responsibly.
Critical Thinking and Problem Solving	(Entire Process)

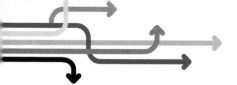

Table 1, Continued.

General Standard	How It Looks in Makerspace (Referenced Back to Problem-Solving Process Poster by Color)
Communication	Students work together to define problems, plan solutions, and finish the problem-solving process. They also communicate what they have learned to the rest of the class. (Entire Process)
Creativity and Innovation	Creativity = Makerspace. A Makerspace is likely the only place in the school where students are free to creatively explore their own ideas without being given a numeric grade (hopefully). (Entire Process)
Geometry	Reason with shapes and their attributes, distinguish between defining attributes versus nondefining attributes, build and draw shapes, compose two-dimensional shapes or three-dimensional shapes.
Investigation and Experimentation	Scientific progress is made by asking meaningful questions and conducting careful investigations. Students should develop their own questions and perform investigations when completing challenges.
Science, Technology, Engineering, Art, and Math	So many correlations; see chapters that follow.

each manipulative. Challenges can be simple (e.g., build an animal, build a spaceship, build something in one minute, make a pattern, or build your name with LEGOs). You could even provide a simple calendar for the week or month and include it with the cart to focus students on a specific task each day (see Table 2).

You could also start simple with a nook filled with items such as, but not limited to, arts and crafts supplies, Tinker Toys, and Marble Runs. As you grow your space, you can begin to transform into a full-blown lab with 3-D printers, laser cutters, and hand tools. Remember, no two Makerspaces are exactly alike, and I don't think they should be. Just be resourceful, use what you have, and get started. That's the hardest and most intimidating part. *Just start making!* Makerspaces are as individual as the school communities they serve. Some quotes I can relate to about Makerspaces and believe to be true are included in Figure 4. In the chapters that follow, we will discuss how to start a Makerspace from the ground up.

Remember, regardless of the space, equipment, goals, and students serviced, it's important to start small. Pick a few things you can

Table 2
Sample LEGO Challenge Calendar

Monday	Tuesday	Wednesday	Thursday	Friday
Build a roller coaster.	Build a rocket.	Build the tallest tower you can before it topples.	Build the toughest truck.	Build a boat with a power source.
Build a tree house.	Make an instrument.	Build a flower.	Build an upside-down house.	Make a model of your favorite animal.
Build something that flies.	Build a robot.	Grab a handful of LEGOs, and build something that uses all of the pieces.	Build a bridge.	Build your name out of LEGOs.
Make a new amusement park ride.	Build your dream house.	Make a maze.	Build a tornado shelter model.	Build something that represents a book you are reading.

To invent, you need a good imagination and a pile of junk. —Thomas Edison

The most dangerous notion a young man can acquire is that there is no more room for originality. —Henry Ford

You do have to try, learn, and improve. You do have to put yourself out there and risk failure. But in this new world, you don't have to go bankrupt if you fail because you can fail small. You can innovate as a hobby. Imagine that: a nation of innovation hobbyists working to make their lives more meaningful and the world a better place. Welcome to the maker revolution. —Mark Hatch, *The Maker Movement Manifesto: Rules for Innovation in the New World of Crafters, Hackers, and Tinkerers*, 2013

Makerspaces provide hands-on, creative ways to encourage students to design, experiment, build and invent as they deeply engage in science, engineering and tinkering. —Jennifer Cooper, "Designing a School Makerspace," 2013

Makerspaces are collaborative learning environments where people come together to share materials and learn new skills . . . makerspaces are not necessarily born out of a specific set of materials or spaces, but rather a mindset of community partnership, collaboration, and creation. —Buffy J. Hamilton, "Makerspaces Participatory Learning, and Libraries," 2015

FIGURE 4. Quotes about Makerspaces.

do well and have access to materials for, and do those really well. Each week, month, or year, add more activities and materials. First and foremost, a Makerspace is about the process of making, not the product. Starting small and simple can help with a smooth transition for all and makes it more likely that administration and coworkers will get on board. If you start out in a very overwhelming way, it will likely not be received as well as a more simple initial approach. You can grow each year.

August

Planning Page and Reflections

1. In your own words, define the word *Makerspace*. What will it mean to *you*?

   _____

   _____

2. What does a Makerspace mean to your campus and colleagues? How do your colleagues feel about having a Makerspace on campus? (Not everyone will be receptive; it's okay.)

   _____

   _____

3. How do your administrators feel about having a Makerspace on campus? (Go ahead and ask! Take this book with you.)

   _____

   _____

4. Brainstorm ways your Makerspace can help you cover state and local mandated standards in a broad context for the general subject areas below.
   - English language arts:_____

     _____

   - Science:_____

     _____

   - Social studies: _____

     _____

   - Math:_____

     _____

   - Technology: _____

     _____

Why Are Makerspaces Important?

What do you do in a makerspace? The simple answer is you make things. Things that you are curious about. Things that spring from your imagination. Things that inspire you and things that you admire. The informal, playful atmosphere allows learning to unfold, rather than conform to a rigid agenda. Making, rather than consuming is the focus. It is craft, engineering, technology and wonder-driven. (Thinkers & Tinkers, 2014)

TARGETS FOR SEPTEMBER

- Define *why* a Makerspace is important to you and your campus/district (not what it is).
- Define *why* you believe you need to provide a Makerspace for your students.
- Determine which research on Makerspaces you feel is the most powerful or meaningful for the group of students you service. Can you find more research to validate using a Makerspace?

By now, you might be thinking, "What does the research say about Makerspaces and STEAM? What do students think of Makerspaces?" Research funded by the National Science Foundation (2013) to identify best practices in education showed that students in all types of schools can and do engage in high-quality science, technology, engineering, art, and mathematics using Makerspaces and STEAM programs. These programs build upon students' early interests and experiences and provide opportunities to engage and learn to investigate questions (using hands-on experiences) about the world that they come across in daily life, similar to the way that scientists and mathematicians do (Community for Advancing Discovery Research in Education, 2014).

The U.S. Department of Commerce stated that workers in STEAM fields earn 26% more than their counterparts, and the job growth rate for these jobs is almost double (Langdon, McKittrick, Beede, Khan, & Doms, 2011). In this book, Makerspace will be modeled around STEAM curriculum, based on the idea of educating students in science, technology, engineering, arts, and mathematics using an interdisciplinary and applied approach. STEAM integrates these seemingly distinct disciplines into an interconnected learning model based on real-life experiences, challenges, and application of knowledge. Projects are engaging, and they encourage students to think critically and problem solve individually and in small groups. You will use a variety of hands-on experiments and challenges in a Makerspace. Research has proven that children who engage in scientific activities at an early age, between birth and age 8, develop positive attitudes toward science, build their vocabulary, and are better problem solvers, while meeting challenges and acquiring new skills (McClure et al., 2017).

What Do Students Think About Makerspaces?

Let's look at what students think about Makerspaces. Table 3 includes quotes directly from some of my students, by grade level, when asked about their Makerspace. Many repeated the same answer, but I have only listed it once. Many of the activities students mention

Table 3

What Do Students Think of Makerspaces?

	Grades 1–3	Grades 4–5
Question Asked	What is Makerspace, what have you learned, or what is your favorite challenge or activity we have done?	What is your favorite challenge, problem to solve, or activity we have done, or what have you learned so far?
Student Responses	• How to use the Gravity Maze. • How to use augmented reality with Quiver. • How to define a problem and then use the problem-solving process. • littleBits are hard but fun! • How to make a marshmallow bridge; it was hard. • How to define a problem. • How to code and program. • How to use Dash and Dot. • How to reflect and redesign. • I can really measure. • How to make a model. • The Big Bad Wolf is mean; he eats the pigs if you don't build a strong house. • The Billy goats could cross my bridge and get away from the grumpy old troll because I built it strong. • Tall things need a big wide bottom. • Plan a solution for the piggy houses. • How to problem solve. • How to stack things tall with a good base. • How to build a great bridge of marshmallows and toothpicks. • About the Three Little Pigs' houses and how to build a strong house. • How to build a tall tower and how to make pig houses. • About measuring. • I learned about vertices and edges with Play-Doh and toothpicks.	• Making a pitch for my shoe design for our mock *Shark Tank*. I planned it, created a model of my shoe and box, and gave a pitch using the Vidra App. • Paper Chair Challenge. • Goldilocks Chair Design Challenge. • LEGO Challenges. • Pumpkin Catapults. • Tall Towers. • *Mayflower* ship with blocks as cargo and marbles as pilgrims. Mine sank the first time but not the second. • Marshmallow and toothpick bridges. I learned about bridge types, like the arch, beam, cable stay, suspension, and truss. • Sometimes the first plan doesn't work, and you have to have another one. • Don't give up. • The *Shark Tank* design and pitch. • Always use teamwork. • How to make new stuff. • How to plan solutions for problems. • It's okay to make mistakes. • Having fun while learning. • To build a tall tower you have to have a solid base. • You don't have to use bricks to build stuff. • How to work with a group a lot of the time. I don't like working with them, but I have to. • Testing how good it worked. • How to be a good problem solver.

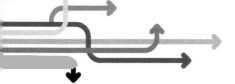

Table 3, Continued.

	Grades 1–3	Grades 4–5
Student Responses, Continued.	• Doodle 4 Google. • LEGO Challenges. • Toothpick and Play-Doh 3-D shapes. • iPad (Osmo Masterpiece and Tangrams). • Pilgrim Dinner Table. • Turkey Hideout. • Cup Towers. • Tall Towers. • Marble Run. • Three Little Pigs and Big Bad Wolf (houses). • Marshmallow Bridge (Billy Goats Gruff). • How to make a structure with candy pumpkins, and we saw who could make the tallest. • How to do LEGO Challenges. • How to draw with Osmo, and the Monster on there is funny. • How to use Bloxels. • How to use the Cubelets. • The newspaper hat challenge. • Making crowns from bending straws. • When we did Quiver. • When we did Hour of Code. • When we made the boats that could float. • The Three Little Pigs, and it was hard to build the houses. • How to make Play-Doh shapes. • Learning while being active. • How to make a marble run that works; it is hard. • How to work together and use our imagination. • How to build with lots of things. • How to make a boat that won't sink. • About edges and vertices.	• If you mess up, fix the problem. • How to make things with what you have on hand. • Teamwork is better than working by yourself. • Work as a group to build stuff. • Measuring. • Cooperate and don't leave anyone out. • We have to work together and get along to problem solve. • How to use littleBits. • Sometimes when you are working in a group, you have to listen to all their ideas. I don't always like that. • How to solve problems. • How to use Dash and Dot. • Make a model. • You can actually use paper to make a chair. • Candy Corn Towers. • littleBit snap circuits. • The tallest building in the world is the Burj Khalifa in Dubai. • Hour of Code. • Marble Run. • Paper, Stick, and Tape Marble Maze. • Doodle 4 Google. • Cup Towers. • Spice Drop Structures. • iPad (Osmo Masterpiece and Tangrams). • Pringles Challenge. • littleBit circuits with light and fan. • Marshmallow Towers. • Newspaper Chair Challenge. • LEGO Challenges. • Tallest Towers. • Foil Boats with Pilgrims (pennies).

Table 3, Continued.

	Grades 1–3	Grades 4–5
Student Responses, Continued.	• Use your imagination. • How to use Dash and Dot and Osmo. • Make fun stuff and work hard. • Do stations like Bee Bots, Osmo Monster, Marble Run, LEGO Wall, and Osmo Tangram. • Build stuff and make stuff. • Create stuff. • Do Doodle 4 Google Contest. • We rotate to stations. • Make slime (simple solutions). • Play Dash and Dot, Osmo Monster, and coding. • Make Marble Runs and keep trying them out. • Do activities to show your parents. • Do the best activity of the whole entire school. • Have so much fun and be amazing.	• Longest Bridge Arch Challenge. • Chess. • Making paper hats. • Dash and Dot. • Hour of Code. • Cubelets. • Bloxels. • Pumpkin and toothpick structures. • Design your own shoe. • Shoebox building. • Marble Run. • Spoon and pumpkin catapults. • Gumdrop Challenge. • Bee-Bots programming and game board. • We use the poster a lot (problem-solving process poster). • Learn about rainforests, volcanoes, and the ocean. • Learn to Code with Hour of Code, Dash and Dot, and Bee-Bots. • Making a 3-D model. I'm still working on it though, and then I can print it on the 3-D printer.

are discussed later in this book. Read the list a second time if you can't see the value of a Makerspace when modeled around STEAM. You can already see how easy it is to weave standards into your Makerspace curriculum, and it is fun. Students often don't realize the extent to which they are learning.

You might get a comment such as, "Those kids are just playing." Consider the following quote, often attributed to Albert Einstein: "Playing is the highest form of research." An abundance of research is available now that children and young adults can learn through play, which can be a reflection of much deeper learning. Students building a house out of LEGOs or completing a LEGO challenge card (see p. 111) together are learning collaboration, engineering, and teamwork. Students designing and redesigning projects to get them just right are

learning about the problem-solving and design process, innovating, and using critical thinking. While sharing the story behind a creation being built, students are expressing storytelling and creativity. These skills help students with academics and for the rest of their lives. That is far more than just play.

Why STEAM Skills?

We know there is a push to develop STEAM skills. Through play and making with manipulatives and objects, such as the examples given in this book, students can learn and understand scientific thinking, and practice math skills, such as measurement, classification, counting, and ordering (Gelfer & Perkins, 1988; Ginsberg, Inoue, & Seo, 1999; Piaget, 1962; Ness & Farenga, 2007; as cited in White, 2015). Even our youngest learners can benefit from Makerspaces. The informal knowledge students gain by experimenting, observing, and comparing while playing and making sets the stage for learning higher order thinking skills and STEAM concepts (Bergen, 2009; Ginsberg, 2006; Shaklee et al., 2008, as cited in Fisher et al., 2011; Tepperman, 2007; as cited in White, 2015). STEAM represents an enormous shift from using standardized test scores, to valuing the learning process. Process over product! Challenge and allow your students to be wrong, to try numerous ideas, listen to different opinions, build, construct, design, discover, generate, invent, make, organize, plan, and produce products that are relevant in real life.

Challenge and allow your students to be wrong, to try numerous ideas, listen to different opinions . . . and produce products that are relevant in real life.

The end product is students who take risks, experiment while learning, display grit while problem solving, work with peers, and work through the problem-solving process. Makerspaces use an integrative and applied approach to incorporate learning standards into a cohesive learning model. This model is based on real-world experiences, challenges, and application of knowledge. Students will be able to tell you what learning standards they have used to accomplish the goal/challenge presented.

According to a report by Langdon et al. (2011), "Science, technology, engineering and mathematics (STEM) workers drive our nation's innovation and competitiveness by generating new ideas, new companies and new industries. However, U.S. businesses frequently voice concerns over the supply and availability of STEM workers" (para. 1). These workers "play a key role in the sustained growth and stability of the U.S. economy, and are a critical component to helping the U.S. win the future" (para. 1). Based on Langdon et al.'s report, compared to non-STEM workers, STEM workers are less likely to experience joblessness and more likely to earn higher wages (26% higher than non-STEM workers). From 2000 to 2010, growth in STEM jobs was 3 times as fast as growth in non-STEM jobs and projected to grow by 17% from 2008 to 2018 (see Figure 5). In 2010, there were 7.6 million STEM workers in the U.S., amounting to about 1 in 18 workers. According to a more recent report (Fayer, Lacey, & Watson, 2017), from 2009 to 2015, STEM employment grew by 10.5% (or 817,260 jobs). In the same time frame, non-STEM jobs only grew by 5.2%. Employment in STEM careers is projected to continue to grow by 6.5% from 2014 to 2024, with the largest growth in mathematical science occupations (think statisticians and mathematicians) by 28.2% or approximately 42,900 jobs. Computer occupation employment is expected to grow by 12.5%, and considering of the size of the existing workforce, this should result in nearly half a million new jobs.

Analysis of data from the U.S. Census Bureau's American Community Survey and Current Population Survey (Noonan, 2017) provides insights into the growing STEM workforce that is central to our economic vitality. STEM jobs are the jobs of the future. They are fundamental for developing technological and global competitiveness. STEM workers are highly desirable to companies developing cutting-edge technology and highly important to the U.S. economy. STEM jobs should be highly enticing to American workers, thus making STEAM a necessary component in Makerspaces. Regardless of educational fulfillment, entering a STEM profession is associated with higher earnings and reduced unemployment. For college graduates, there is a payoff in choosing to pursue a STEM degree, and for America's workers, an even greater payoff in choosing a STEM career

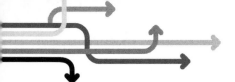

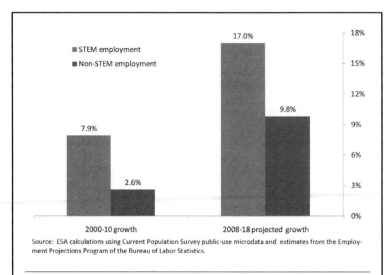

Source: ESA calculations using Current Population Survey public-use microdata and estimates from the Employment Projections Program of the Bureau of Labor Statistics.

FIGURE 5. Recent and projected growth in STEM and non-STEM employment. From *STEM: Good Jobs Now and For the Future* (p. 1), by D. Langdon, G. McKittrick, D. Beede, B. Khan, and M. Doms, 2011, Washington, DC: U.S. Department of Commerce Economics and Statistics Administration.

(Langdon et al., 2011). Figure 6 compiles some related research into an infographic for easy visualization.

Regardless of whether today's students work in technical careers, become doctors or politicians, or whatever they choose, we know that with the challenges their generation will face, they will be expected to be problem solvers who are educated in science, technology, engineering, art, and math and have excellent soft skills. STEAM is gaining attention in government and research as well. With universal competition rising, America must rethink its economic future. STEAM education is an opportunity for U.S. workers to be the innovators, creators, and technical leaders of the world. This is a pivotal point for Americans. Makerspaces are the perfect fit for this type of learning to occur.

STEAM education is an opportunity for U.S. workers to be the innovators, creators, and technical leaders of the world.

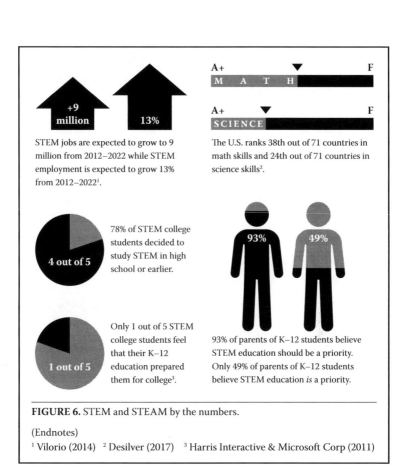

FIGURE 6. STEM and STEAM by the numbers.

(Endnotes)

[1] Vilorio (2014)   [2] Desilver (2017)   [3] Harris Interactive & Microsoft Corp (2011)

Studies have shown (e.g., Khan, 2015) that the technology industry will grow at an unprecedented rate, and we'll need workers who can code, designers who can problem solve, and innovators who can understand what we need before we even need it. The solution is a greater emphasis on STEAM education. I believe we must start in elementary school. We must teach and encourage creative and critical thinking and problem solving. When we think of science, technology, engineering, arts, and math, we think of exploration, critical and creative questioning, problem solving, and the engineering design process. According to James Brown, the executive director of the STEM Coalition in Washington, DC, "The future of the economy is in STEM. That's where the jobs of tomorrow will be" (as cited in Hill, 2017, para. 2). I fully believe he is correct.

Enough Research Already!—How Do I Talk to Other Teachers and My Administrators?

I do not give you all of this research to bore you. I want you to feel empowered when asking to start a Makerspace or create a Makerspace nook in your classroom or library. Most budget decisions are guided by research. Ask your administration or school board to please read at least the first two chapters in this book. Hopefully they will be open to reading the rest.

Q: How do I talk to my principal and other administrators about why a Makerspace is important?

A: Show them the data. STEAM jobs are not being filled at the rate they are being created. A majority of our students will work in jobs that don't even exist yet, and Makerspaces modeled around STEAM address this problem.

The U.S. News/Raytheon STEM Index showed that STEM employment in the United States increased by more than 30%, from 12.8 million STEM jobs (as defined by the U.S. government) in 2000 to 16.8 million in 2013 (U.S. News & World Report, 2014). But those numbers do not include jobs in nontraditionally STEM fields that still require STEM skills.

"Perhaps we ought to shift from asking 'how many STEM workers do we need?' to 'what knowledge and skills do all of our workers need to be successful now and in the future?'" Kelvin Droegemeier, vice chairman at the National Science Board and meteorology professor and vice president for research at the University of Oklahoma, said in a statement accompanying the report. "Millions of workers who aren't typically understood to be 'STEM workers' need these capabilities to be successful, and businesses need individuals with these skills to be globally competitive."

Regardless of what degree or trade our students pursue, they must be digitally proficient. Providing our students with opportunities to fine-tune these skills is expected. Makerspaces are the perfect places to incorporate these opportunities with other subject areas in a cohesive way. Students can document their learning through various digital platforms. I will go into detail about this in later chapters.

So often with technology, we think as teachers that we have to be 100% proficient in the technology we are giving to our students. We do not. It's perfectly fine to say, "I just got this in (or I just found this cool app). I haven't figured it out yet. Can you help me?" Trust me, students will be honored you asked and appreciative that you are honest. We don't have to have all of the answers. It's okay to learn with our students or even learn from them. According to data from the U.S. Bureau of Labor Statistics (2013), employment in occupations related to STEM is projected to grow to more than 9 million between 2012 and 2022. That's an increase of about 1 million jobs from 2012 employment levels. This is the future for our students. We cannot continue to educate them in the ways of the past. We must move forward with our students.

It's okay to learn with our students or even learn from them.

All students should be qualified to think passionately and creatively so that they have the chance to become the innovators, educators, researchers, and leaders who can solve the most pressing issues facing our nation. As it stands, not enough of our students have access to quality STEAM learning opportunities. We have to help students see the connection between STEAM and future careers so they can flourish in our present-day STEAM economy. The United States is falling behind internationally in STEAM preparedness. We can be enthusiastic in response to this by improving STEAM instruction in Pre-K–grade 12. We can do this by connecting the growing structure of educational disciplines. STEAM provides an incredible opportunity for teaching how interconnected subjects relate to real life. STEAM education can be more gratifying, purposeful, and engaging when compared to traditional ways we educate children. Educators can write STEAM lessons to match the national and state-level benchmarks and standards that testing systems expect us to cover.

Why Provide STEAM Experiences?

All students should have the opportunity to be able to learn in the ways that coordinate with their cognitive ability and what they are passionate about. Makerspaces with STEAM are a way to organize and utilize best practices and ideas, as well as customize learning experiences for students involved. STEAM education is research-based and proven to be effective. Makerspaces allow students to study and observe first, without the fear of getting something wrong, and encourage confidence and risk-taking in the classroom. What a perfect combination.

Typically, students feel pressure to get the answer right or to make a good grade. What happens when they are presented with a challenge that does not have one right answer? At first, this can actually be scary for them, but as you create an atmosphere of warmth, compassion, and a safe place where it's okay to mess up and try again, you will see aspects of your students' cognitive and social abilities that you just cannot see in the regular classroom setting. More often than not in Makerspaces, students jump in and start trying new things and taking risks, which is something you don't always see in other subject areas. In order for students to be willing to take risks in your room, you must first build a relationship with them. Let them see you try and then mess up. Show them you are human, too, and make mistakes. It is okay. When students trust you, the progress that unfolds using the problem-solving process is amazing to watch.

In order for students to be willing to take risks in your room, you must first build a relationship with them. Let them see you try and then mess up.

The problem-solving process (see Figure 2, p. 16) will provide vertical alignment within your campus or district, as it becomes common language with your students. This will empower your students to work through any problems or challenges they might face by using this simple process. Ideally, posters should be provided for all classrooms and posted in common areas.

Makerspaces are creative spaces. Allowing our students time to be creative and innovative can reduce stress and anxiety for our students. Being creative taps into the right side of the brain (Families. com, n.d.). This means anxiety and depression sufferers can benefit from lower stress and anxiety levels while being creative. I had a student who, at times, struggles with anxiety tell me, "Coming here feels like a second counselor." I asked her what she meant by that, and she said, "After I leave I feel calmer and happier!" Makerspaces support students' social and emotional needs (see Table 4) and help them find their passions—how great is that?

According to Alice Sterling Honig of Syracuse University (as cited in Preble, n.d.), "The great engine that drives innovation and invention in society comes from people whose flame of creativity was kept alive in childhood. Research shows that, if not nurtured, creativity takes a nosedive by fourth grade" (para. 5). Often, this happens in classrooms. We teach students to give answers we want rather than find the answers themselves. Makerspaces are set up in a manner that forces students to find the answer by being a problem solver. Learning how to be more creative causes kids to become more adaptable and prepares students for life beyond school.

In his popular TED talk, Ken Robinson (2006) made the powerful point that most of the students in your classrooms today will be entering a job force that none of you can visualize. That talk is from more than 10 years ago, so we already know he was right, and he'll continue to be in the years to come. So let's get started making your Makerspace.

Keep Making

As we begin to dig deeper into Makerspaces modeled around STEAM, please know that lessons do not require expensive equipment, special classrooms, or large spaces. Don't become overwhelmed at the thought of what this space must look like. Expectations are great, but be open to lowering your expectations on what your space must look like or have in it, and raise your expectation to focus on the process of making. Remember: Process over product. Again, no two Makerspaces are the same, and that is great. You can start a

Table 4
Social and Emotional Outcomes of Makerspaces

Better academic performance
Improved attitudes and behaviors: Greater motivation to learn and deeper commitment to school
Fewer negative behaviors: Decreased disruptive class behavior
Reduced emotional distress: Less depression, anxiety, stress, and social withdrawal
Self-awareness/recognizing emotions and thoughts • What are my strengths given this particular making task? • What are my limitations, and how can I use my strengths to overcome them?
Social awareness: Being aware of the perspectives of and empathizing with others • Am I listening and understanding others' perspectives?
Self-management/regulating emotions, thoughts, and behavior: Developing and revising goals and managing frustrations • What processes am I using to develop and revise my goals while making? • What strategies am I using to manage frustrations and failures?
Relationship skills: Communicating clearly, listening actively, cooperating, collaborating, resolving conflicts, and seeking and offering help when needed • How am I using others to help me with my project? • How are my peers and I collaborating? • Am I asking for help if and when I get stuck making my project? • How am I sharing my ideas with others?
Responsible decision making/making good choices about personal behavior and social interactions • What am I doing to keep my peers and myself physically safe during the making of my project? • What are the consequences of my actions on my peers and myself while making my project? • What past projects are informing my decisions for this project?

Makerspace with everyday household items that parents and staff can donate. Virtually, you can get started for free, along with some innovation on your part. This book is designed from the beginning to work in any educational program, during the regular school day or in after-school programs, camps, etc.

If you search online for "STEAM lessons" or "Makerspace lessons," you will not come up short. I will not be using this book to give you a list of lessons to use. You can find those all over the Internet and through networking, both of which you should continue to do. What you cannot find easily is how to actually make a Makerspace work for you. I will give example lessons, photos, and a sample 6-week scope and sequence I have used, but my goal is for you to see the process. Once you have that down, Makerspace lessons and activities are much easier to present and, most importantly, implement. You can pick and choose from a variety of lessons to find ones that you can adapt for your students and customize for state standards, school expectations, etc.

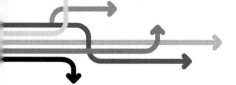

September

Planning Page and Reflections

1. Why is a Makerspace important to you and your campus/district (not what is it)?

   _____

   _____

   _____

   _____

   _____

   _____

2. Why do you believe you need to provide a Makerspace for *your* students?

   _____

   _____

   _____

   _____

   _____

   _____

3. What research from Chapter 2 do you feel is the most powerful or meaningful for the group of students you service?

   _____

   _____

   _____

   _____

   _____

   _____

4. Can you find more research to validate using a Makerspace at your school? Write down what you find here.

   _____

   _____

   _____

   _____

   _____

   _____

CHAPTER 3: OCTOBER

Makerspace Planning and Wonder Walls

The secret of getting ahead is getting started.

—Mark Twain

TARGETS FOR OCTOBER

- Complete the Makerspace Planning Sheet (at the end of this chapter). This is pretty in-depth and will take some time to thoughtfully complete.
- Start your Wonder Wall. (There is a sample provided in this chapter.)

As maker education grows in popularity, many educators want to incorporate this type of learning into their classrooms or schools. Makerspaces create a critical thinking environment and provide collaboration and teamwork. Activities should be crossdisciplinary, which is where STEAM comes into play. We all know schools are already on very tight budgets. When planning, a key factor to keep in mind is that your Makerspace should encourage learning through play, experimentation, innovation, and creativity. You can do all of this in a very low-tech Makerspace, as well as in a high-tech Makerspace or a Makerspace that falls somewhere in between low- and high-tech (as most do).

The main focus of this chapter is in the planning pages at the end of the chapter. These pages are highly important because they will give you direction for your Makerspace as you move forward. Although this chapter is short, the reflections and activities at the end will take a little more time than other chapters. Plan to spend more time than usual at the end of this chapter.

Before Jumping In

Before I started making specific plans for how my Makerspace would operate, I read everything that I could get my hands on that would inform me and help me make good decisions when planning. I read online, researched other schools, classrooms, and communities that had Makerspaces, read blogs about Makerspaces, and followed makers on Twitter. Even though I have a Makerspace up and successfully running, I am still constantly seeking information that will improve my students' experience. It is an ongoing process. You're off to a great start with the first two chapters of this book. You can also refer to the additional resources in the Appendix for more Makerspace research and ideas, and always be on the lookout for new ideas.

Organizing Your Makerspace

If you have a dedicated space for making, ideally you need long tables so kids can spread out and work. But use what you have. Ask to look in the storage space for your district furniture and see what's there. You can cover old tables with butcher paper to give students a place to plan. Students can work on the floor as well. They will need defined work areas, planning areas, and places to display work if possible.

How you will organize your space regarding material storage is dependent on the space available to you. You can search online and find a plethora of ways (e.g., search for "Makerspace storage ideas" on Google and/or Pinterest). If you have an unused room or closet, etc., on campus, this would be a great place to store items you are not currently using. Many items that you will ask for on your donation list (see p. 95) will require storage space until you are ready to use them. Plan for this. If you do not have storage, a solution would be to request a week in advance only the donations you will use the next week. This makes your Makerspace a much more structured environment, but it is better than nothing. Again, work with what you have.

Q: Makerspaces are messy. How do you keep control of the classroom?

A: Just like in a traditional classroom, rules, routines, and expectations have to be in place, practiced, and enforced. Students need to know where items can be found, how to use them, and how to clean up appropriately before leaving the Makerspace.

Consumable Materials Storage

I am lucky to have an empty room across the hall from my classroom. I store my items there. I have buckets and bins to sort materials and then a large area to store boxes, plastic containers, etc. If you have a parent volunteer who wants to help, having him or her come every other week to put donations away and sort materials would be a great idea. The storage aspect can quickly become overwhelming if you don't have a plan in place to address organization at least every other week. This is a continual task. I've included some photos of my storage area, before being organized and after (see Figure 7). It's nothing fancy, but it is organized (75% of the time), so I know what we have and what we need more of.

Nonconsumable Materials Storage

In my actual Makerspace classroom, I store all of my nonconsumable materials. I use white plastic bins to contain materials, as well as caddies and big storage tubs. Supplies are returned to the same spot *every time*, so students know how to clean up our space. This is very important—just like in a traditional classroom setting. Students need to know where to find supplies and where to return them. I like to place visual posters and reminders for items, such as electronic devices like Bee-Bots and littleBits, to name a couple. These visuals are hung low on the wall, and when we use these materials, the students automatically know what area they are to use the items in. Providing visual reminders about how to use items helps students take ownership of getting started right away and working as a team to use the visuals provided. For example, in my classroom, we have LEGO Wall, which includes peel-and-stick LEGO building plates (see Figure 13, p. 59). They stick directly onto the wall (or could stick to a piece of plywood if a wall is not an option) for students to build upon. For our LEGO Wall, challenges are stored directly beside the wall in a pocket chart. Figure 8 includes some photos for some ideas on storage and defined work areas with visuals.

Create, Not Consume

You can offer interdisciplinary exploration and creation with very few materials. Students must be led to create and not to consume. This will greatly help your budget and allow your materials to last longer. So many challenges can be made even more challenging by requiring students to only use a certain amount of materials provided. This asks students to be more innovative and creative, most likely in a way that is very different than if they had access to an unlimited amount of materials. If they need tape, for example, tell them how much they can use (e.g., "You may use up to four 1-foot pieces of tape," or any other unit of measure you need students to work with). Have them measure it. Otherwise, you will run out of supplies *very fast*.

Before   After

FIGURE 7. Before and after organizing consumable materials storage.

Flexible seating opportunities in the classroom.   Classroom cabinet storage.   Nonconsumable material storage bins.

Bee-Bot station.   littleBits station.

FIGURE 8. Storage and work area ideas.

45

Q: What are some ways teachers can model maker behaviors and mentalities for students?

A: Makerspaces are about the maker culture, not the space. Use what you have, and encourage students to use what's available to them to innovate and create. Let students see you fail and see you be wrong. Let students know you don't know it all and that's okay . . . reflect and redesign!

Enhance and Contribute to Core Classes

Begin to think of how you can enhance and contribute to what is happening in your students' core classes. As testing time approaches on campus, and even before and after that time, check with teachers and find out in which areas students are struggling. If it's math, how can you help cover vertices and edges or area and perimeter in a playful, planned, and purposeful way? For grade levels working on life cycles, how can you integrate this topic into your Makerspace? For high school students, while studying the solar system, students could choose one planet and create an extraterrestrial that could survive under the conditions of that planet. The list can go on and on. If available, get a scope and sequence from each grade level you will work with, and use that as a springboard for ideas. A few detailed ideas follow.

Sample Vertices and Edges Activity

For vertices and edges, making 2-D and 3-D shapes with toothpicks (edges) and Play-Doh (vertices) might very well be what makes these two vocabulary words click for many students. Actually building and forming the structures can provide an amazing tactile anchor. Figure 9 shows some of my students working on this activity. The recording sheets students are using are by Playdough to Plato, available on Teachers Pay Teachers (https://www.teacherspayteachers.com/Product/STEM-Challenge-Build-Toothpick-Structures-2712959).

Area and Perimeter

For area and perimeter this year, I asked my husband for blueprints from jobs he has completed and no longer needs (this could be a great addition to your donation list; see p. 95). My students and I used these to make area and perimeter meaningful (adults actually use these concepts) and also something they can relate to (most blueprints are for jobs in the vicinity around your town). To make this even more fun, use your projector and/or computer and Google Earth or a similar application to view the actual building you will be measuring. You can use blueprints for many math objectives, including computing actual lengths from a scale drawing, elevations, area and perimeter, basic views of objects, meaning of commonly used lines on a blueprint, basic dimension conventions, decimal tolerances, precision measuring, blueprint terms used in the title box and note column, symbols commonly used in company blueprints, metric and customary units, and angle measurement, etc.—so much better than a worksheet. Laminate the blueprints to use over and over again. Figure 10 includes photos of my Makerspace class using blueprints. These were a smaller version. We used larger ones as well.

Ideas for Life Cycles

Could students use your space to plant seeds and "window watch" as they grow? Great seed choices are lima beans, sunflower seeds, marigolds, or alfalfa sprouts. Soak the seeds overnight to speed up the germination process if desired. Have students use damp paper towels or cotton balls (eight or so) and place them in a Ziploc bag with a few seeds. Tape these to the window and have students observe. Students could take a photo each day and use the movie app Stop Motion Studio to make a stop motion video of the seeds growing. They could also use paper, clay, or playdough to "make" the life cycle being taught, each in his or her own unique way.

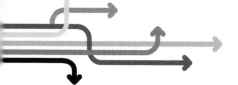

FIGURE 9. Sample vertices and edges activity.

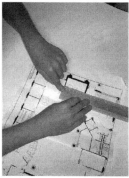

FIGURE 10. Students working on an area and perimeter activity using real-life blueprints.

Ideas for Extraterrestrials and Planets

For this activity, I would leave the choices fairly open as for how students will "make" the extraterrestrial and demonstrate what makes it unique so that it can survive on the planet chosen. Let students know that they have to be specific on the planet choice, demonstrate why and what the extraterrestrial "needs" to survive, and also make a model.

Wonder Walls: I Wonder About and What if...?

Wonder Walls are another great way to develop ideas that your students will find relevant and meaningful. I like to build a Wonder Wall as soon as possible when school starts. A Wonder Wall is as simple as it sounds. Ask students, "What do you wonder about?" Then record their wonders. I have included a picture of our Wonder Wall after the first week back in August and midway through the year around December (see Figure 11). The students have so many topics they wonder about. You can provide sticky notes for students to add wonders anytime they have one. The wall will grow all year long and become a springboard for providing activities that interest, captivate, and cause your students to be curious and want to learn. Another idea is to add a section to your wall with the prompt "What if...?" Figure 12 includes examples from our Wonder Wall from grades K–5.

As students start to wonder, be mindful of eliminating the fear of failure for you and your students. As you start, give yourself permission to take risks. Really, what is the worst that can go wrong? Not all of your activities are going to work out. Not all of your students' ideas and projects will work out. It's okay. Work to remove the fear of failure. Keeping your focus on the process and not the product will help with this.

Work to remove the fear of failure.

To encourage students and let them know failure is okay, videos from Kid President are amazing and inspirational. Check out his videos at http://kidpresident.com. They can motivate students and teachers to be the best they can be and live up to their full potential. Students will love his videos, which you can start or end your Makerspace time with.

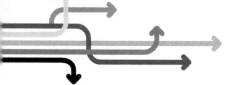

Classroom Wonder Wall in August.

Classroom Wonder Wall in December.

FIGURE 11. Sample classroom Wonder Wall at the start of the school year and halfway through the school year.

I wonder . . .

What my mom does while I'm at school

If aliens are real

What challenges we will do this year

How cats see in the dark

Why I am addicted to electronics

If I can make a robot

How cars work

About hurricanes

About space

About the ocean's depth

If I can have more summer break

Who invented a baseball

Why do dogs bark during storms

Why we wonder

Why there are so many animals in the world

Who created the word *wonder*

Why spiders are even alive

What the future is like

What it would be like to be in the 1990s

If all my friends I have now will still be my friends

Why is there so many people

If there is a robot that can do your laundry

When I'm going to see my dad

When I'm going to be able to cook

If there will be flying cars in the future

If I'll get a treat after school

What I'm going to do at baseball practice tonight

What the next day is going to be like

What I'm going to eat for dinner

How football will be in the future

Who created marbles

Who will be the first lady president

Why people can't fly

Why dinosaurs were made

If animals can understand us

How I can build a drone

How old my brain is

How the world works

FIGURE 12. Sample responses from a Wonder Wall for grades K–5.

Keep Making

Be mindful that as you begin, not everyone will appreciate or understand why you are creating a Makerspace or even understand what the word means. Those who are skeptical or hesitant will learn by watching you. Remember to focus on the process, not the product.

Work through the problem-solving process with your students. The Maker Movement is a perfect match for schools because of its natural connection with STEAM. Making is about learning, providing evidence of what you learned, and reflecting. We have to move away from the "sit and get" approach to teaching. They may sit, and some may get . . . but this type of rote learning simply isn't practical or fun to do all day at school. Let's make school fun again. Our goal must be to let students be actively engaged in the learning process. A Makerspace will help you accomplish this goal.

October

Planning Pages and Reflections

1. Why are you building a Makerspace? What are you looking to get out of both the process and the space?

   _____

   _____

2. Which students/grade levels will use your Makerspace? How often will they come? Who will staff the Makerspace?

   _____

   _____

3. Where will your Makerspace be . . . a nook in your classroom, a spot in the library, an empty classroom? Remember to use any space available; don't wait for the perfect place. It might require your school to reprioritize its use of space. Write down several possible places.

   _____

   _____

4. How soon do you foresee yourself implementing your Makerspace?

   _____

   _____

5. What is your plan for getting your administration and coteachers on board? How will you involve all stakeholders? Remember to try to include teachers, students, parents, community members, school board members, and administration. (Chapters 1 and 2 have research-based answers should you need them.)

   _____

   _____

Continues on next page . . .

6. Which materials are you already thinking of using? The list of tools and materials will consistently grow as you do projects and activities. Anticipate needing additional space as your program grows. What materials does your school already have that can be used in your Makerspace? A list of detailed materials will be provided in later chapters, but think about what we have covered so far and what you already have that you can use.
   - Can implement soon: _____
   - Plan to implement in the future: _____
     _____
     _____

7. What tools do you want to include?
   - Can implement soon: _____
   - Plan to implement in the future: _____
     _____
     _____

8. How will you establish a maker culture in your classroom, school, or district? How can you share what you are doing with other teachers? (Idea: I have a photo/idea link on my school webpage that is updated often so parents and community members can see what we do. I also present at faculty meeting or staff development days when asked and to our school board to showcase what we do.) How can you share what you are doing outside of your classroom?
   _____
   _____

9. As soon as possible, start your Wonder Wall and/or What If . . .? Wall. Where will you put your Wonder Wall and/or What If . . .? Wall, and how will students add to it as they have new wonders throughout the day?
   _____
   _____

10. How will you store and organize your materials as you get them and/or they are donated? Can you think of a parent or community member who would help sort your materials?
   _____
   _____

Developing and Implementing Makerspace Activities

However, don't let perfectionism become an excuse for never getting started.

—Marilu Henner

TARGETS FOR NOVEMBER

- Plan six simple and inexpensive/free activities to implement.
- Implement the activities you have planned. Plenty of ideas are given in this chapter to get you going; don't worry!

Makerspace Teachers as Facilitators and Encouragers of Learning

Makerspace teachers are truly facilitators and encouragers when lessons are set up well. A Makerspace activity certainly requires more work on the front end, but during the lesson, you can interact, provide guidance and suggestions, ask leading questions, and observe. Try not to limit your students by the margins of your knowledge base. Don't expect to be the expert in your Makerspace. It's okay to not know it all. Challenge your students, and then get out of the way.

Is What You're Planning Feasible and Realistic?

I want you to feel like you can get started with providing students with more easy-to-implement but challenging Makerspace activities after reading this chapter. I am going to provide some simple ideas to help you get going in the sections that follow. I see so many great activities and challenges in books and online, but the reality is that when you are servicing 30 or 300+ students a week, an awful lot of what you see will not work for large groups because of the expense of needed items, the need for a one-to-one environment to complete activities, and time constraints. When you are planning activities, it's important to ask yourself if what you are planning is realistic and feasible for the number of students you will serve. Keep your challenges obtainable.

Q: What does your Makerspace look like?
What materials get used the most?

A: It varies from week to week and from grade level to grade level. Focus on the process, not the product or materials, and you will get students excited regardless of what materials you have.

Simple Challenges You Can Use Now

Gather simple supplies (free, donated, garage sale), and develop simple challenges using them. An easy way to begin is by having students rotate through 5–6 stations that include materials and challenges, such as popsicle sticks, LEGOs, Marble Run, K'Nex, wooden blocks (e.g., KEVA planks), newspaper for paper construction challenges, magnetic blocks for building and measuring, and/or materials for building the tallest tower. These items should be fairly simple to find on campus or ask parents to donate. It can be that simple, and then you can grow your Makerspace from there. The following sections include descriptions of several challenges and photos of students participating in these easy-to-implement activities. Several also include example problem-solving processes to illustrate how simple it is to implement these activities.

Popsicle Bridge Challenge

A simple way to start is to have a Popsicle-stick bridge challenge. Craft sticks are great for young innovators and makers to create with. A huge box is very cheap, and the sticks can be used over and over again. A sample problem-solving process is included below.

Define the Problem or Challenge: Build a bridge that will hold up a small metal car and that spans a certain gap (provide students a ruler and the minimum size the gap must be) and can support the weight of the car. Use books as risers.

Plan Solutions: Work with your team to discuss and draw out a plan.

Make a Model or Plan a Strategy: Provide small metal cars from the dollar store and have the students create a bridge using the books and craft sticks.

Test the Model or Try It Out: Place the car on your bridge. What happens?

Reflect and Redesign: If the bridge worked, why did it work? If it did not work, what do you need to change? Try it out!

LEGO Challenges

Students can use any LEGOs available to complete challenges (see the sample LEGO challenge calendar on p. 19 or ready-to-use challenge cards on p. 111). Figure 13 shows some of my students working with LEGOs.

Marble Runs

Marble runs can be plastic, wooden, or homemade. You can buy the plastic and wooden varieties. Marble runs require students to connect pieces correctly to allow the marble placed at the top to travel all of the way to the bottom without stopping. Having students create a marble run using recycled materials is a challenging and cheap activity that I have used in my Makerspace for the past 2 years and have found to be extremely successful. In the sample problem-solving process below, note how students are given firm parameters as far as what materials they can use and also have to measure the tape they use. They are also given a goal for the amount of time the marble should actually run. There are lots of challenges there. See the complete lesson below. Figure 14 includes some photos of my students working with marble runs.

Define the Problem or Challenge: Make a marble run using the materials and parameters given.

Plan Solutions: You may only use two cardboard boxes, scissors, 15 craft sticks, four paper rolls, tape (three 3-foot strips maximum—measure), and marbles. Your marble must run at least 5 seconds, the longer the better. Who can make his or her marble go the longest amount of time? Brainstorm for 5 minutes (verbally or draw).

Make a Model or Plan a Strategy: *You may begin!*

Test the Model or Try It Out: Test as you work and when you finish.

Reflect and Redesign: If your marble run works, talk about why it works. If it does not work, how can you fix it? Try it! When you finish, get an iPad and video your marble running for at least 5 seconds.

FIGURE 13. Students working on LEGO challenges.

FIGURE 14. Students working on marble run challenges.

K'Nex Challenges

You can buy large and small K'Nex. These can connect in a variety of ways as a construction activity (see Figure 15).

Wooden Blocks or KEVA Planks

You can buy KEVA planks or use any wooden blocks or even Jenga blocks to build with (see Figure 16).

FIGURE 15. Students working on K'Nex challenges.

FIGURE 16. Students working with KEVA planks.

Tallest Tower Challenge

Supply plastic cups, marshmallows and uncooked spaghetti, playing cards, Play-Doh, and toothpicks—the list is endless—for students to construct the tallest towers that they can. You can even provide real-world photos of tall structures for student inspiration. A sample problem-solving process is included on the following page, and Figure 17 shows some students working on a Tallest Tower Challenge.

Define the Problem or Challenge: How can you build the *tallest tower*?

Plan Solutions: Does a tower need to have a wide base or a skinny base in order to be sturdy? Let's look at nature for a clue. Stand on one leg and balance. Now stand on two. Which is easier? Two legs because it makes your base bigger. How about a Christmas tree? The bottom is wide, and the top is narrow. What are other items in nature that you can think of that have a wide base? Talk to your group.

Make a Model or Plan a Strategy: Build with your materials.

Test the Model or Try It Out: Test as you work.

Reflect and Redesign: What worked, and what didn't? Why? How would you change your design if you were to do this again?

FIGURE 17. Students working on "Tallest Tower" challenges.

Magnetic Blocks

You can buy magnetic building blocks from a variety of vendors. They are flat blocks that have magnets inside. Thus, they easily connect to each other and provide many opportunities for building challenges (see Figure 18).

Cardboard Challenges

If you only have cardboard boxes, you can get started. Have a cardboard challenge. I promise, you'll be very surprised at students' cre-

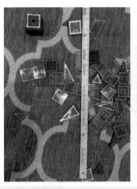

FIGURE 18. A student working with magnetic blocks.

ative process. Watch Caine's Arcade (http://cainesarcade.com) to help get your students' creative juices flowing. A sample problem-solving process is included below, and Figure 19 includes photos of a few of the cardboard activities my students have done.

Define the Problem or Challenge: What can you make with recycled cardboard? Use tape, glue, and cardboard to see what you can design and create.

Plan Solutions: Discuss and draw out potential ideas.

Make a Model or Plan a Strategy: Build, create, and make.

Test the Model or Try It Out: This task is open-ended, so you will test as you work.

Reflect and Redesign: What worked, what didn't, and what would you do differently next time?

Building Upon Simple Challenges

Integrating Technology and Coding

If technology is more your thing and you want to start simply with that, try coding. Although even the word "coding" can seem intimi-

FIGURE 19. Students working on cardboard challenges.

dating, there are several easy-to-use resources and apps for introducing students to coding that don't require you to be an expert and don't require expenses other than tablets. I use Hour of Code (https://hourofcode.com) and love it. Truly, it is one of the simplest ways to let students learn to code. You commit to letting each student code for one hour, and then they receive a certificate at the end of the hour. They can pick from a ton of coding modules, and again, the goal is the process, not the product. Simply ask your students to try. If you're still nervous about coding, just trust me, and let your students try it.

A few other easy-to-use tools include Scratch (https://scratch.mit.edu), Scratch Junior (https://www.scratchjr.org), and Daisy the Dinosaur. They are all designed for teaching coding using visuals—plus, they are easy to learn and free. There are many coding books for kids as well. Figure 20 is a photo of one of my students coding using one of these books. Google "coding books for kids" or see the Appendix (p. 175) for a short list of coding resources. Other hands-on ways for students to code include using Bee-Bots (https://www.bee-bot.us) or Dash and Dot robots (https://www.makewonder.com). These robots and other devices are discussed further in Chapter 10.

You can also introduce your students to the world of 3-D printing using a platform such as Tinkercad (https://www.tinkercad.com). Even if you don't have a 3-D printer, students will still learn plenty by making 3-D models and working through the basic tutorials and moving to harder activities when they are ready. Tinkercad is very self-explanatory. Give it a try; you won't be disappointed.

FIGURE 20. A student learning to code.

As you start using technology in your Makerspace, if you don't have a device for each student, don't worry. You can have students work together in small groups as needed. I'll share other ideas for technology integration in later chapters.

Using Literature

Children's literature can be a great starting point for STEAM challenges in a Makerspace. *The Three Billy Goats Gruff* leads naturally to bridge challenges. *The Three Little Pigs* lends itself to engineering homes to keep the pigs safe from the big bad wolf. *Goldilocks and the Three Bears* is an excellent starting point for engineering a new chair to replace the broken one in the story. The list is endless. You can virtually create a challenge for any children's book you use with your class. If you are not feeling creative enough to come up with your own, you can search online for many ideas. This is applicable for older students as well, using novels or units of study. For example, in a Makerspace, an English teacher could have students create something that represents a theme or character from the most recent book they have read. Alternatively, you can have students develop their own challenges based on ideas presented in novels or units of study.

The Popsicle bridge challenge discussed in the previous section could easily be adapted for the story *The Three Billy Goats Gruff*. You might find that literature is a comfortable starting point for you. Use your imagination! Here is a lesson for this activity that correlates with the problem-solving process. Figure 21 includes a few pictures from our activity. Remember to substitute items as needed—just use what you have.

Three Billy Goats Gruff Toothpick and Marshmallow Bridge Challenge

Define the Problem or Challenge: Build a bridge using only marshmallows and toothpicks.

Plan Solutions: How will you hold up your billy goat and keep him safe from the mean old troll?

Make a Model or Plan a Strategy: You can use marshmallows and toothpicks in any manner you wish. (*Teacher's Note*. For older students, give a specific length that the bridge must span, and have them measure it, or give a specific weight it must hold and have them use small weights to test it. Fishing weights work great for this and are cheap.)

Test the Model or Try It Out: Have fun using your structural engineering skills as you test your model as you work.

Reflect and Redesign: Redesign your bridge if it does not work. If it works, why was it successful?

Introducing QR Codes for Self-Driven Learning

I wanted my students to learn how to use a QR reader and also be making at the same time. There are a number of QR reader apps available, and iOS devices have a QR reader integrated into their cameras. The lesson I presented to my students combined the use of QR codes on iPads and origami. If you have never created a QR code for students to use, search online for information on how to create a QR code. It is so easy. I used the URL http://www.origami-fun.com/origami-for-kids.html to link to the QR code for this lesson. Figure 22 includes the lesson I used in my Makerspace.

QR Codes are also great to have on display for early finishers to scan and have activities to choose from without needing your immediate attention. Figure 23 is an example of the poster I have in my room.

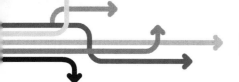

FIGURE 21. Students working on the Three Billy Goats Gruff toothpick and marshmallow bridge challenge.

Origami for Kids

1. Get a tablet and scan the QR code (open QR scanner).
2. Pick an origami that interests you.
3. Grab some paper and get started.
4. You may work by yourself or in groups of 2–3.
5. Have fun making. We will present at the end of class!

FIGURE 22. Origami for kids lesson using a QR code.

Early Finishers Websites/QR Codes

http://msbolotin.wixsite.com/kbkonnectedkids

https://sites.google.com/a/bosquevilleisd.org/
mrs-brejcha-s-class/student-resource-page

FIGURE 23. Sample early finishers poster.

Keep Making

You're off to great places! Today is your day! Your mountain is waiting so . . . Get on your way!
—Dr. Seuss

I have given you many ideas, but don't feel like you have to implement them all. Remember to use what you have on hand and value the process over the product. Get creative with substituting materials you have access to.

November

Planning Pages and Reflections

Plan six easy, simple, inexpensive (or free) activities to implement in November, and then implement them this month. Plenty of ideas are given in this chapter to get you going; don't worry.

Activity/Challenge #1

Activity/Challenge Name:_____

Supplies Needed:

_____
_____
_____
_____
_____
_____

Process/Plan:

_____
_____
_____
_____
_____
_____

Standards Covered:

_____
_____
_____
_____
_____
_____

Continues on next page . . .

Activity/Challenge #2

Activity/Challenge Name:_____

Supplies Needed:

_____
_____
_____
_____
_____
_____

Process/Plan:

_____
_____
_____
_____
_____
_____

Standards Covered:

_____
_____
_____
_____
_____
_____

Continues on next page . . .

Activity/Challenge #3

Activity/Challenge Name:_____

Supplies Needed:

_____
_____
_____
_____
_____
_____

Process/Plan:

_____
_____
_____
_____
_____
_____

Standards Covered:

_____
_____
_____
_____
_____
_____

Continues on next page . . .

Activity/Challenge #4

Activity/Challenge Name: _____

Supplies Needed:

_____

_____

_____

_____

_____

_____

Process/Plan:

_____

_____

_____

_____

_____

_____

Standards Covered:

_____

_____

_____

_____

_____

_____

Continues on next page . . .

Activity/Challenge #5

Activity/Challenge Name:_____

Supplies Needed:
_____
_____
_____
_____
_____

Process/Plan:
_____
_____
_____
_____
_____

Standards Covered:
_____
_____
_____
_____
_____

Continues on next page . . .

Activity/Challenge #6

Activity/Challenge Name: _____

Supplies Needed:

_____
_____
_____
_____
_____
_____

Process/Plan:

_____
_____
_____
_____
_____
_____

Standards Covered:

_____
_____
_____
_____
_____
_____

Providing Assessment and Recording Standards

Learning is the only thing the mind never exhausts, never fears, and never regrets.

—Leonardo da Vinci

We do not learn from experience . . . we learn from reflecting on experience.

—John Dewey

DECEMBER TARGETS

- Devise a way to record standards that are covered during each Makerspace lesson.
- Create and/or decide on an assessment strategy for your Makerspace.

A Makerspace is a place where you will do far more formative assessment and reflection, rather than using other types of assessment tools. This chapter includes a variety of assessment and documentation strategies, as well as strategies for putting students in charge of their learning, which are all fairly simple and quick to utilize. Any of the tools described or a combination of them should be more than sufficient to document the problem-solving process that is taking place every day in your Makerspace. You might find that something else works better for you, and that is great as well. Do what works for you and your students.

Q: Does Makerspace have to be tied to your curriculum, or can it go beyond that?

A: I think a mix of both provides a great balance for students' and administrators' expectations. Balance is key!

As the strategies in this chapter will make clear, you can record standards covered in Makerspace in a variety of ways. But please note: You don't need to grade everything. Learning still happens even if it's not graded. Take lots of photos and upload them to your webpage for parents and the community to see. Use the app Remind (https://www.remind.com) or ClassDojo (https://www.classdojo.com) to communicate with parents about the projects going on in your room. If you use Google Classroom, you can communicate this way as well. Other ideas include newsletters, polls, and surveys. These are wonderful ways to document learning without a grade. Although assessment and standard documentation can be integrated, learning in a Makerspace is informal for the most part.

Utilizing Authentic Assessment

Make certain that any assessment you use in Makerspace is an authentic assessment. Be sure your assessments replicate real-world challenges. These are the types of tasks our students will need upon graduation and in their careers. Makerspaces require unique assessment methods, as a Makerspace is not the same as a traditional classroom. It is important to acknowledge gains students make in soft skills and problem-solving skills. Assessments should be content- and performance-driven.

Journals and Reflections

For a written assessment, one option is to use a journal reflection (see Figure 24) for students to record and document the problem-solving process as they work. You can make each student a journal and use a handout like this as the cover or inside cover, and students can use the same spiral all year to record answers. At the end of the year, they will have a wonderful portfolio to take home. Figure 25 shows a different example of a journal that uses reflection through emotions. Students document what they made, and then, using emoji, they document how they felt while they were making the project. Lastly, they draw a picture of what they made. The emotion journal works well for younger learners.

Graphic Organizers and Rubrics

Figure 26 is an example of a graphic organizer for reflection. Students use a visual flow chart organizer to show what they made, how they made it, why they made it, and what it looks like. They conclude with what they would change if they did the project again. Figure 27 is an example of a rubric that looks at students work through three different angles (grading myself, grading my team, and then a teacher evaluation rubric). This allows students to get feedback from multiple sources as well as give feedback to their peers and themselves.

Simple Questioning That Ties Into State Testing

You can tie in questions for reflections and class discussion that relate to state standards fairly easily. For the challenge "Create Your Own Marble Run" (see p. 58), questions might include:
- If the marble flies out of the tubing rather than continuing down the track, something needs to be altered. Which variable is causing the problem?

Problem-Solving Process Journal	Name:_____ Date: _____ Homeroom Teacher: _____

Journal Reflection:

1. What was the problem or challenge?
   _____

2. How did you plan solutions, and who did you plan with?
   _____

3. What did you do to make a model or plan a strategy?
   _____

4. When you tested your model or tried out your strategy, did it work? What happened?
   _____

5. Take a moment to reflect on what went well and what you would change if you did this challenge again.
   _____

Problem-Solving Process diagram:
- Define the Problem or Challenge
- Plan Solutions
- Make a Model or Plan a Strategy
- Test the Model or Try It Out
- Reflect and Redesign

FIGURE 24. Sample problem-solving process journal reflection pages.

Name:_____ Date: _____

What I Made: _____

How I Feel About What I Made:

Happy   Sad   Confused/Unsure   Love

Draw a picture of what you made:

[ ]

FIGURE 25. Sample feeling/reflection journal.

Name: _____ Date: _____

Makerspace Graphic Organizer

What did you make?

How did you make it?

Explain why you made it.

What does it look like? Draw it here.

What would you change if you did this project again?

FIGURE 26. Sample reflection graphic organizer.

- What is energy, and how is it related to motion?
- How is energy transferred?
- How can energy be used to solve the problem?

Exit Tickets

Before leaving the Makerspace, have students turn in a "ticket" filled out with an answer to a question, a solution to a problem, or a response to what they've learned. Technology offers an easy way to use exit tickets. You can search online for "exit tickets" and find many options. Some ideas include using Poll Everywhere (https://www.poll everywhere.com), Plickers (https://www.plickers.com), or Google Forms. Students can easily use a tablet, smartphone, or computer to fill out exit tickets. These apps can immediately compile the information for you. Paper and pencil are a great option as well. This requires more teacher effort to collect responses, but still gives you assessment information. Question/prompt ideas for exit tickets include:

- Share one thing you learned.
- Share a question for a future challenge.

Name: _____   Date: _____

Rubric

	Unsatisfactory Effort (0 points)	Effort Needs Improvement (1 point)	Satisfactory Effort (2 points)	Amazing Effort (4 points)
Grading Myself	I contributed to the teamwork.			
	I used the problem-solving process.			
	I was positive and pleasant to work with.			
	I completed the task to the best of my ability.			
	I made sure to reflect and redesign.			
Grading My Team	We worked pleasantly together.			
	We used the problem-solving process.			
	We were positive and polite.			
	We completed the task to the best of our ability.			
	We made sure to reflect and redesign.			
Grade From My Teacher	Student used the problem-solving process.			
	Student completed the task using teamwork.			
	Student was pleasant and positive to work with.			
	Student completed the task to the best of his or her ability.			
	Student reflected and redesigned.			

Notice we are focusing on the process/effort, not the final product!

FIGURE 27. Sample rubric.

- Respond with a word, phrase, or sentence about today's activity.
- What worked?
- What didn't work?
- What is one part of your challenge that you are proud of?
- How would you change your plan next time?

Student-Led Conferences

Students can lead conferences to share reflections, goals, how they used the problem-solving process, and their progression. Conferences can be with peer groups or in addition to parent-teacher conferences.

Anecdotal Records

Write down informal descriptions of a student's progress involving a specific problem or area of difficulty in Makerspace. The record is a result of a direct observation. Anecdotal records can be used to document student achievement.

Application Cards

After a task or challenge, ask students to write down one real-world application for what they have just learned. "Real-world" is the key here.

QR Reflection Codes

These are so simple to use. Search online for "QR Reflection Codes," and you will have plenty of choices. Print your choice of codes, and when it's time for students to reflect, have them scan a Reflection QR Code. These are so simple and easy to use. Questions might include:
- What was most challenging?
- What helped your learning?
- When something got hard, what did you do to help yourself?

Turn and Tell

Have students turn and tell a friend the answer to a question you ask. It's just that simple. This is great for quick reflection when you are out of time. You can do this while students are in line waiting for the next transition to leave your classroom, switching classrooms, taking breaks, etc.

Putting Students in Charge of Documenting Learning

Each challenge or activity should include a documentation or presentation component if time allows. Often, I like to have students use different apps as a way to document and think about what they are doing. Some examples involve having students use the comic strip maker app Strip Designer (http://vividapps.com/Strip_Designer). When I introduced *Mayflower* projects with my fourth graders, the students used Strip Designer to document their learning. I gave fairly simple guidelines: Take a picture of your team while you come up with a plan, while you make your model, while you try it out, and then while you fixed your boat if it had a problem. (*Note.* These steps come straight from the problem-solving process.) Figure 28 includes a couple of photos of the students' documentation of learning. They made these by themselves and then e-mailed them to me from their iPads.

When you look over creations that students make while documenting their work, it allows for a different insight into their thinking and their ideas. You will discover what they think was important and great about what they made. On the following page is the entire lesson. You can use it right away (for a printable student resource, see the book's webpage at https://www.prufrock.com/makerspaces-in-school-resources.aspx).

FIGURE 28. Student documentation of learning.

Mayflower Boat-Building Challenge

Background Information

Search for an appropriate video on the *Mayflower* that works for the age group you are doing the activity with. Tell students that the *Mayflower* sailed to America in 1620. The boat traveled across the Atlantic Ocean with 102 passengers, cargo, and crew. The construction of the *Mayflower* had to withstand the fierce weather on the ocean but also carry the weight from the additional passengers and cargo.

STEAM Skills Presented/Objectives

Science: Students will use the problem-solving process for planning and constructing the boats and testing the constructions to see if they can float and hold weight.

Technology: Students will document learning through use of technology by taking photos and videos.

Engineering: Students will plan and construct a boat that exhibits early attempts at engineering from simple supplies.

Arts: Create a mini-*Mayflower*.

Math: Explore mathematical relationships while planning, constructing, testing, and improving the engineered boats. Measure while working to stay within the measurement constraints given and use standard units of measure (marbles and blocks).

Problem/Challenge

The students' challenge is to plan, design, and create a mini-*Mayflower* using the criteria and constraints below.

- Boats must float in the water tub.
- Boats must hold at least five Pilgrims (five marbles) and two cargo packs (plastic blocks); more is better.
- Boats may *not* be longer than 7 inches or wider than 5 inches (measure).
- Students do not have to use all of the supplies, but no additional supplies will be given.
- The time limit for planning and construction is 25 minutes. Students may test their designs as they work and make improvements if desired or needed.
- Students should take a video or photos of their products (being careful with the iPads and the water). If they have time, students can make a photo strip on the Strip Designer app.

Materials Allowed

- 10 craft (Popsicle) sticks
- 5 sticky notes
- 5 toothpicks
- Aluminum foil
- Tape
- Tub for float test
- Scissors
- Ruler
- 5+ marbles
- 2+ cargo packs
- One challenge card
- iPad (at the end—if you don't have iPads, skip this—no worries)
- PowToon review on iPad (AirPlay mirroring—if you don't have Apple AirPlay, skip this. A document camera could substitute as well. Again, use what you have.)

Plan Solutions

Students should sketch their design ideas with their groups on a whiteboard or a piece of paper, discussing solutions and how they will make their model.

Make a Model or Plan a Strategy

Start the challenge.

Test the Model or Try It Out

Have students test as they work.

Reflect and Redesign

Have students redesign as needed while they work. When they are finished, have students use an iPad to take photos or a video of their final product and present to the class (technology).

Challenge Wrap-Up (Whole Class, Verbally)

Ask students:
- If you built another, what would you change and why?
- If you could add one new material for a future design, what would it be and why?

I also used the same documentation process for our Tallest Tower Challenge. The students rotated to four different stations, each with a different material to build with and had to take a picture and insert it into their team's photo strip. I made groups of four or fewer students in each so each child had a turn to use the iPad and experience the app. Figure 29 includes photo strips that my third-grade students made by themselves. They were so proud to show off their photo strips of what they had done. By adding this simple documentation method, you not only cover the standards in the lesson but also cover many technology standards as well.

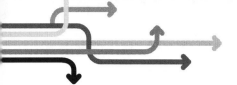

FIGURE 29. Student documentation of learning.

Shark Tank-Style Pitches

When we did our *Shark Tank* pitches in fourth and fifth grade, students were given the option to present their project using Google Slides, Vidra (http://tentouchapps.com/vidra), iMovie, Canva (https://www.canva.com), Book Creator (https://bookcreator.com), Strip Designer, or another app of their choosing with prior permission. Just like on the show *Shark Tank*, these pitches require students to convince their peers, "the sharks," to "buy" the product they have designed. The presentations all varied, but each had to meet the same requirements as far as what information was communicated.

What I Learned Board

Make a board somewhere in the classroom or Makerspace area and label it "What I Learned." Provide sticky notes for students to continually add what they have learned after each challenge they have completed or after their Makerspace time. This is an easy place to collect students' thoughts on what they feel like they have learned. This helps them take ownership of their learning.

Pre- and Post-Activity Surveys

Use a simple platform like Survey Monkey (https://www.survey monkey.com) or Google Forms to record students' knowledge before and after challenges and activities. Use the same platform to have them reflect on what they have learned. Pre-activity questions might include:

- What do you want to learn more about?
- What do you want to understand how to do?
- In what areas do you want to develop your skills?

Post-activity questions might include:

- What were the most important learning points for you?
- What did you gain a better understanding of?
- In which areas did you improve your skills?

Documenting Standards

You can document standards covered in several ways. One way is for students to document in their journals what objective, state standards, and/or performance objectives they used for that particular day. Another way to mix it up a little is to give students standards for each week from each subject area and have them see if they can apply these to their Makerspace projects/challenges. Alternatively, you can plan specific Makerspace challenges to address any standard(s) of your choosing. I like to include objectives/standards directly on my lessons as they are displayed on the interactive projector so students can see them as we discuss an activity.

If you need to cover measurement, for example, you can have students measure the towers they build using whatever unit of measure you need to cover. You can have them convert units of measurement while doing this same task. For public speaking and technology, have students create a presentation using a technology presentation app and have them verbally present it to the class using your document camera, interactive whiteboard, or Apple TV. If you don't have these, they can present straight from their tablet, desktop, laptop, or poster. Again, use what you have.

Observation

As students work through documenting learning using the ideas given on the previous page, walk around to observe and take note of the words you hear them saying. These most always can be tied into a standard. If you use the problem-solving process and practice becoming a facilitator during this time, you can take many notes and make many observations that will truly amaze you.

Shifting From Passive to Active Learners

It is important to note that the role of the learner changes in a Makerspace from a more passive learner to an active, creative problem solver. We, as teachers, should encourage creativity and design so students learn new skills and feel comfortable and confident to create, make, and innovate. A Makerspace is a unique place for creativity and design. Curriculum is not delivered and followed by a test or standard assessment. Instead, we must examine our assessment and evaluation practices currently in place. We must find a better solution to support our students.

We, as teachers, should encourage creativity and design so students learn new skills and feel comfortable and confident to create, make, and innovate.

I love the "What I Learned" board because this is a wonderful way to show standards that are being met and it comes straight from the kids. You can transfer these boards to a recording sheet for your records. I would keep a running list of standards met for every 6 weeks (or 8 weeks depending on your district). Figure 30 is an example of a simple chart to record standards on that is broken down by general subject areas.

Name:_____ Date:_____

Standards Recording Chart

Makerspace Standards Covered During: _____
Teacher Name: _____

Subject	Standards Covered
ELA	
Social Studies	
Math	
Science	
Technology and Digital Citizenship	
Art	
Communication	
Problem Solving and Critical Thinking	
Constructing, Designing, Creativity, and Innovation	

FIGURE 30. Sample standards recording chart.

Keep Making

As you move forward, remember, you do not need to formally assess the majority of work that happens in Makerspace. The process and the products, along with using the problem-solving process, should provide plenty of meaningful opportunities for observation.

December

Planning Page and Reflections

1. Create or decide on an assessment strategy for your Makerspace. Use the space below to plan this or make your own. If you like ideas presented in this chapter, add page numbers here. Don't forget to include soft skills assessments in addition to other skills. Remember, we must prepare our students for the real world, using authentic assessment.

_____

_____

_____

_____

_____

2. Plan or create a strategy for documenting standards covered in your Makerspace. Use the space below to plan this. How will you document to your administration, etc., what your students are learning and why?

_____

_____

_____

_____

_____

3. If you would like to use a similar recording chart to the one that I use, you can design one here to meet your needs for your students:

Being Resourceful

Requesting Donations for Materials, Getting Helpers or Outside Experts, and Help... We Don't Have Room for a Makerspace!

It's not the lack of resources that cause failure, it's the lack of resource-fulness that causes failure.

—Tony Robbins

Alone we can do so little, together we can do so much.

—Helen Keller

JANUARY TARGETS

- Determine how you will ask for donations for your Makerspace and what you will include on your donation list.
- Decide how you will get the community on board for materials requests.
- Determine the funding options for your Makerspace.
- Decide how you will use outside experts and community helpers in your Makerspace.
- Brainstorm alternative spaces for your Makerspace if you do not have a dedicated place and/or how you will set up your space.

Acquiring Consumable Materials

A Makerspace program requires many consumable materials. Figure 31 includes a list of practical donation ideas. Many of the items you will need parents will likely have at home. You might need volunteers to help organize and sort your materials depending on how large your space is. In your reflection and planning pages for this month, you have a space to make a donation list and to add additional items you want to request. I have also added a list of items that may not be as practical but may be something you want to try to include as you grow your Makerspace.

Q: If finances are low, what are the most critical pieces to include in a Makerspace?

A: You can start for free. A donation list is included in the book that consists mostly of donated recycled items. From there, pick items that are presented in this book or other resources you find relevant for your unique space.

Funding Options

Some ideas for funding your Makerspace are listed below. Be thinking of additional options that are accessible in your community.

- **Grants:** You can find a large list of educational grants on Edutopia (https://www.edutopia.org/grants-and-resources). You can also look at your state's education agency website for available grants.
- **DonorsChoose.org projects:** DonorsChoose.org is a funding site for public schools. It guides you through every step of every project, and upon your project being funded, DonorsChoose.org purchases each item and ships materials directly to your school. Visit https://www.donorschoose.org for more details and to apply.
- **Local business donations:** Businesses are often willing to donate when they know of a specific program or need that they feel is beneficial to students. If you need a donation of

- Rolls of masking tape
- Scotch tape
- Craft supplies
- Cardboard
- Plastic materials
- Paper
- Styrofoam
- Paint
- Collage materials
- Rainbow Loom
- Knitting and crochet supplies
- Duct tape
- Boxes of uncooked spaghetti noodles (thicker spaghetti noodles)
- Plastic cups (all sizes)
- Coffee filters
- Q-Tips
- Eye-droppers
- Vinegar
- Baking soda
- Ping-pong balls
- Play-Doh
- Marshmallows
- Plastic silverware
- Cotton balls
- Felt
- Small, rubber bouncy balls
- Pipe cleaners
- Cardboard tubes (toilet paper and paper towel tubes)
- Poster board
- Empty and clean cardboard containers
- Aluminum foil
- Saran wrap
- Wax paper
- Matchbox cars (to keep)
- Small action figures (to keep)
- Flexi straws
- Toothpicks
- Marbles
- Paint sticks
- Finished blueprints (for measurement activities)
- Milk jug and/or water bottle caps
- Large Ziploc bags (all sizes)
- String (yarn, twine, fishing line)
- Small pebbles or rocks
- Rubber bands
- Metal washers (various sizes)
- Egg cartons
- Popsicle sticks (large and small)
- Wood scraps (generally smaller pieces)
- Dowels
- Styrofoam
- Zip ties
- PVC pipe (generally smaller pieces)
- Wire

Other Very Useful Donations Include:

- LEGOs
- Tinkertoys
- K'Nex
- Marble Run
- Wooden blocks
- Flashlights
- Clear plastic bins

FIGURE 31. Sample Makerspace donation list ideas.

a specific type of material, and a local business stocks it, ask the business if it would be willing to donate. I make sure that I publicly thank any business that donates to us through social media, such as on Twitter or Facebook, and also send a thank you note from my students and myself.

- **Students' family/staff donations:** Family and staff are great people to ask for items on your recyclable consumables list. These items are free; you just need people to save the items for you as they use them.
- **PTA/PTO funds:** Inquire with your PTO or PTA about available grants.
- **Student activity account funds:** Ask your principal about the availability of these funds.
- **Fund raisers:** I like to use the website Fundly (see https://blog.fundly.com/fundraising-ideas-for-schools-and-education) to research fundraiser ideas for schools.

A sample letter for parents that I have used is included in Figure 32. After students have visited Makerspace once or twice, I like to send this note. If you are starting from the ground up, send this home to parents as soon as you start planning.

Inviting Outside Experts

Outside experts can be extremely helpful and encouraging as your students work on various projects. Technology can bridge the gap between experts and classrooms. You can accomplish this by using Skype or any video chat platform. Nepris (https://www.nepris.com) is a great tool for finding outside expert connections. Nepris (2013–2018) "provide[s] teachers the tools to connect curriculum with the real world by virtually inviting industry professionals into the classroom to engage and inspire students in STEAM!" (para. 1). Nepris does cost, so that might be a roadblock to an otherwise neat program. You can also use Twitter, Facebook, Pinterest, Google +, YouTube, and other social media forums to find outside experts and/or ideas in general for your Makerspace.

Makerspace Parent Information Letter

Dear Bosqueville Elementary Parents and Guardians,

My name is Lacy Brejcha. I will be the Makerspace teacher again this year. This is my 16th year to teach at Bosqueville Elementary, and I am looking forward to continuing to implement our Makerspace Program that will service *all* students in grades K–5! You are most likely wondering . . . what is a Makerspace? I have attached some information to explain this new program and my expectations. I will see all classes in grades 1–5 every week for 45 minutes and kindergarten every other week.

Makerspace will be modeled around STEAM curriculum, based on the idea of educating students in science, technology, engineering, arts, and mathematics using an interdisciplinary approach. Rather than teach these areas as separate and discrete subjects, STEAM integrates them into a cohesive learning model based on world experiences, challenges, and application of knowledge. Projects are engaging, and they encourage students to think critically and problem solve individually and in small groups. We will use a variety of hands-on experiments and challenges when your child comes to Makerspace. I could not be more excited!

In order to offer this program, we require an abundance of consumable materials. Attached is a list of ways you can help us. Many of the items we need you may already have at home. *All donations can be taken to the office.* If you have any questions, please don't hesitate to contact me. You can find my contact information on my webpage at https://sites.google.com/a/bosquevilleisd.org/mrs-brejcha-s-class. (My site is a work in progress; check back often for updates!) Remind 101 information will come home soon so you can get my class messages. I will need volunteers to help organize and sort our stock room. If you can offer your help in this way, please let me know.

All the best,
Mrs. Brejcha

What Is a Makerspace?

A place to . . .

- Create stuff
- Learn how to do something new
- Do arts and crafts
- Build things
- Be challenged
- Have fun
- Solve puzzles
- Problem solve
- Explore
- Open your imagination
- Draw
- Build things
- Make things
- Play games
- Write
- Be creative
- Participate in challenges
- Have choices of things to use
- Use a ton of awesome technology

FIGURE 32. Sample parent information letter.

Makerspace Expectations

- Be respectful and use kind words.
- Work together.
- Include everyone; don't exclude.
- Be proactive and make good choices.
- Use the problem-solving method (all 5 steps!).
- Follow directions.

- Take care of all equipment and supplies.
- Help clean up all areas.
- Don't take materials.
- Listen to each other.
- Be calm and use good manners.
- Share all materials.

FIGURE 32. Continued.

Online Videos

Online videos are another great way to bring the real world to your classroom. You can find videos that would be meaningful to show your students for virtually any project, challenge, unit of study, or content area. Obviously, preview videos carefully from beginning to end before showing them to your students. The goal is for students to see people in the real world using the skills you are expecting them to master.

Business, College, and School Partnerships

A business partnership is another great way to get experts into the classroom. Making a connection with a local university might be of interest as well. Graduate and undergraduate students would be an excellent bridge from the classroom to the real world. If your students are in elementary or junior high, high school students might be an option. For instance, with LEGO Robotics, your high school LEGO Robotics team would be wonderful mentors for your elementary or junior high LEGO Robotics team.

Other Inspirational Ideas: An Extensive List of Items You May Want to Add as You Grow Your Space

The following list gives more ideas of materials and activities you may want to add to your space as you grow your space over the next weeks, months, or years. All of the ideas can be open-ended or structured with task-specific cards. Note that I am not an expert in all of these areas, and you don't need to be either!

- **Make it and take it:** Supplies for bookmarks, greeting cards, and seasonal crafts that students can make in their Makerspace and take home the same day
- **Duct tape creations and designs:** Duct tape of any variety and pattern
- **Jewelry making:** String and beads to create necklaces and bracelets
- **Sewing and stitching:** Knitting, crocheting, embroidery, and needlepoint supplies; sewing machines; looms; cross-stitching kits; quilt-making patterns and materials; fashion design inspiration and fabrics
- **Paper and modeling:** Paper and clay for origami, foldables, paper airplanes and gliders, gift wrapping, Play-Doh, pottery-making supplies
- **Apps, software, and web-based tools:** Tablets/computers with apps for comic making, animations, photo editing
- **Video production:** Tablets/cameras, production space or room, green screen, Movie Maker, iMovie
- **Graphic design:** Canva, Adobe Photoshop, Adobe Illustrator, and Adobe InDesign
- **Cooking:** Cookie-decorating and cake-decorating supplies, recipes, cooking supplies
- **Writing:** Washable markers, permanent markers, chalk, pencils, crayons, erasers, oil pastels
- **3-D modeling and printing:** 3-D printer, 3Doodler pen
- **Electrics:** Batteries, battery packs, wire, LEDs, hobby motors, toothbrushes, vibrating motor, electronic snap circuits

- **Building parts:** Cable ties, brads, zip ties, craft sticks, rubber bands, screws, string, nuts and bolts, straws, pipe cleaners
- **Tools:** Wire cutters, hammers, screwdrivers, pliers, tape measures, scissors, rulers, any and all
- **Paint:** Tempera, watercolor, spray, acrylic, paint palettes
- **Brushes:** Large and small paintbrushes, foam brushes, sponges
- **Adhesives:** Glue, glue guns, glue sticks, tape (all kinds), staplers, magnets
- **Safety equipment:** Goggles, gloves, lab coats, fire extinguisher
- **Paper:** White, colored, card stock, watercolor, cardboard scraps, coffee filters, origami paper
- **Embellishments:** Googly eyes, sequins, beads, glitter
- **Cleaning and organization:** Sponges, bowls, soap, trays, paper towels, baby wipes, disinfecting wipes, containers, jars

Building Inspirations: A List of Items Students Can Build With

- Wooden blocks
- Magnetic blocks
- Paper rolls
- Aluminum foil
- Containers
- Books
- Pipe cleaners
- Rocks
- Cups
- Pasta noodles and marshmallows
- Spools
- Foam
- LEGOs
- Toothpicks and spice drops, gum drops, marshmallows
- Play-Doh
- Straws
- Sticks
- Cans
- Playing cards
- Popsicle/craft sticks
- Cotton swabs
- Marble Runs
- Plastic caps
- Index cards
- Yogurt cups
- Egg cartons
- Foil baking tins
- Air-dry clay
- Tubing
- Greeting cards
- Small wood pieces
- Packing peanuts
- PVC pipe

- Bowls
- Magnets
- Milk cartons

- Coffee cans
- Oatmeal containers

But ... I Don't Have Room for a Makerspace!

If you do not have a dedicated Makerspace on your campus, you can still implement a Makerspace. A Makerspace is more about the attitude and approach to learning more so than the space. Ideas if you don't have a separate space for your Makerspace include: a nook in your classroom, mobile engineering carts, libraries, or even portable laundry baskets. Again, start small and add on as you go. Perhaps members of your grade level team can each make a Makerspace basket and have a circulating Makerspace. You can put it in a nook in your classroom and rotate weekly with your team. It can truly be that easy.

Keep Making

Once you get started, it will be easy to build momentum. After your school sees how awesome a Makerspace can be, it may consider reuse of a currently used space that would be better suited for Makerspace along with possibly taking another look at the current budget to help fund Makerspace.

January

Planning Page and Reflections

1. Come up with a plan to ask for donations for your Makerspace. Use the space below to plan and decide how you will ask for donations from parents and the community. How will you get the parents and community on board for materials requests?

   _____

   _____

   _____

2. What are some ideas you have for funding options in your community? Also list potential places (businesses, etc.) that you can ask for donations from or buy items very cheap from.

   _____

   _____

   _____

3. Make your donation list below.

   _____

   _____

   _____

4. Think of outside experts and community helpers that you could contact to visit your Makerspace and be a mentor or share something new: Brainstorm a list of potential people below.

   _____

   _____

   _____

5. If you don't have a dedicated Makerspace, plan alternative places and ideas here:

   _____

   _____

   _____

Keeping a Makerspace Planned, Playful, and Purposeful

Creativity is intelligence having fun.

—Albert Einstein

FEBRUARY TARGETS

- Plan three thematic Makerspace units that are purposeful, planned, and playful. How will you implement them?
- Select books that will encourage creation, innovation, and problem solving.

As you continue to plan how your space is structured, starting with a thematic unit can be helpful. I do not mean your typical thematic units, but broad topics of challenges for students, such as a unit on:

- coding,
- paper challenges,
- pipe cleaner challenges,
- Popsicle stick challenges,
- aluminum foil challenges,
- duct tape challenges,
- LEGO challenges, or
- cotton swab challenges.

You can plan to focus on a broad topic for about 3 weeks, assuming you see classes for about 45 minutes. If you have a nook in your classroom, you might provide two bins and have two different broad topics to choose from.

This is where task or challenge cards can come into play. The best way I have found to run my Makerspace using these broad topics is to provide task cards for each material. These task cards inspire students to use provided materials to complete a challenge, such as making a circuit with littleBits that lights up and makes a horn beep. I provide some sample task cards in this chapter, but you can easily develop your own or search online to find more than you will ever need. If for each broad topic you have 12 or more challenge cards, students can complete four challenge task cards each week. Depending on how much time you have for Makerspace, this will vary. You can easily find 25 LEGO task cards and leave them out for 3 weeks for students to complete at their own pace. Also, students love coming up with challenges for their peers after they have become familiar with the materials being used. If you see students who seem ready to move on, let them create task cards for the materials you are providing, and let them offer those to their peers.

Q: What are some tips you would offer teachers to help guide students rather than leading them through projects?

A: Challenge them and then get out of their way. Use the problem-solving process and allow students to peer teach and collaborate. Facilitate as students are highly and actively engaged.

Introducing Task Cards to Students

Task cards are motivating for students because there is only one task per card, specific learning objectives are made clear, they make differentiation come naturally, they are versatile, and they help bring focus to your Makerspace. Task cards allow you to observe what students are doing, and the task they are to complete is very clear to you, your students, and anyone who comes into your space.

Sample Coding Task Cards

For a unit or set of Makerspace activities on coding and computer sciences, I am going to recommend that you use the Scratch Cards available at https://scratch.mit.edu/info/cards. Here you will find a lot of task cards that help students learn Scratch Coding. I also recommend Hour of Code (https://hourofcode.com). I have participated with my classes in Hour of Code for the last 2 years and, because Hour of Code allows you to award students with certificates for each hour they complete, I was able to give 285+ hours of coding awards during both years. It was amazing; the students loved it. Both the Scratch Cards and Hour of Code are very easy to implement and are great ways to get students making if they have access to tablets or computers.

If you do not have access to tablets or computers, there are "unplugged" activities you can do with coding. Visit https://code.org/curriculum/unplugged. This site has compiled a list of unplugged lessons. You can teach the fundamentals of computer science without tablets or computers. This website has many activities to choose from for ages 4 and up.

Any of these activities could easily last 3 (or many more) weeks to give directions and cohesion to your Makerspace. Coding encompasses so many tools, including robots, coding apps, coding books, and Hour of Code, to name a few. Students will want ample time to explore more than one coding platform. Each student will most likely pick a different challenge within the coding unit. That is great! This is what we want. Students can find their passion within the unit if given choice.

Ready-to-Use Task Cards

Sample task cards are provided in this section. These tasks are all ready to use. You just need to create the cards, or you can find downloadable versions on the book's webpage (https://www.prufrock.com/makerspaces-in-school-resources.aspx).

Paper Challenge Task Cards

- Make a party hat using one sheet of paper and 4 inches of tape.
- Build a boat using one sheet of paper.
- Make the tallest structure you can, using three sheets of paper and 12 inches of tape.
- Create a playground slide using three sheets of paper and 6 inches of tape.
- Design a bridge that spans a minimum of 6 inches, using paper and tape.
- Design an envelope that can hold paper, using only paper and 6 inches of tape.

Note. I put measurements on tape for three reasons. The first is so students have to measure. Secondly, they will use all of your tape immediately if you don't. Third, it makes the challenge even more challenging. Figure 33 includes some photos of students at work on paper challenges.

Newspaper Challenge Task Cards

- Design a hat that you can wear, using only newspaper and 6 inches of tape.
- Make a jump rope and see if it works.
- Make a shirt that fits you and then decorate it.
- Build the tallest tower you can with only newspaper and 12 inches of tape.
- Make a cube using only newspaper and 12 inches of tape.
- Make a gift bag using newspaper and 12 inches of tape.

FIGURE 33. Students working on paper challenges.

Pipe Cleaner Challenge Task Cards

- Create a model of an insect (including a head, a thorax, an abdomen, six legs, and antennae).
- Construct a chain that is longer than you.
- Design a birdcage.
- Make a hat or crown that fits your head.
- Make a basket with a handle that can hold a _____ .
- Create a wheel that can roll.

Note. Figure 34 includes some photos of pipe cleaner challenges.

Wooden Clothespins, Binder Clips, and Craft Sticks Challenge Task Cards

- Build a structure that can support the most weight possible.
- Build the tallest structure you can, then measure the height in inches.
- Build the tallest structure you can with the least amount of clothespins.
- Build a bridge that can hold _____ ounces. (*Teacher's Note.* Fishing weights work great and are cheap.)
- What can you build with triangles?
- Design a house for the three little pigs.

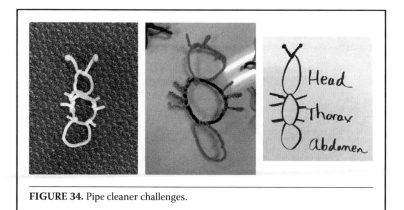

FIGURE 34. Pipe cleaner challenges.

Tin Foil Challenge Task Cards

- Create a sculpture of a person.
- Design a picture frame.
- Make a boat that can float while holding 10 marbles.
- Construct a model of a house.
- Make jewelry, watches, or something you can wear.
- Design and make an umbrella or other device to keep you dry.

Note. Figure 35 includes a photo of students working on a tin foil challenge.

Duct Tape Challenge Task Cards

- Create a duct tape wallet.
- Design a duct tape pencil case.
- Make a duct tape pen.
- Design a duct tape water bottle holder.
- Create a duct tape keychain.
- Make a luggage tag for your suitcase.

FIGURE 35. Students working on a tin foil challenge.

LEGO Challenge Task Cards

- Make a LEGO bridge.
- Create a model of a dinosaur.
- Make an upside-down house.
- Make a LEGO car that can roll.
- What can you build in only 30 seconds, 1 minute, 2 minutes . . . ?
- Make a LEGO marble maze.

Cotton Swabs Challenge Task Cards

- Using 12 inches of tape, construct a teepee that can stand on its own.
- Make a house complete with a roof using 12 inches of tape.
- Construct a three-dimensional cube using 12 inches of tape.
- How many different figures can you create with only 10 cotton swabs and 12 inches of tape?
- Construct a model of a dog pen, using 12 inches of tape.
- Make a model of a piece of playground equipment, using 12 inches of tape.

Children's and Adolescents' Books to Inspire Makerspace Thinking

To inspire students to begin thinking, innovating, problem solving, creating, taking risks, and be willing to fail, an inspirational children's book can be very beneficial. This section includes a list of picture books to help motivate your younger students and also books to motivate your older makers. Any or all of these books are a great way to connect through literature that it's okay to make mistakes, be creative, and be innovative, and that if you stick with your goal, it will most likely eventually happen. You can start your Makerspace session at the beginning of the year by reading a different one of these books each week with younger kids. Leave them out all year for your students to return to if they desire. With older kids, most books are more project-based and will help them find what they are passionate about and enjoy doing.

The Most Magnificent Thing by Ashley Spires (Elementary Ages)

The Most Magnificent Thing is a picture book about a girl and her best friend, who is a dog. The girl has a wonderful idea to make the most magnificent thing. She thinks she knows how it will look and work. She makes things all the time, so it should be easy. But, as she begins to make, it isn't so easy after all. She tries and fails more than once. After becoming angry and giving up, her dog convinces her to take a walk, and when she returns, she has a new perspective and completes her most magnificent thing. This book helps students value the rewards that come from persistence and creativity.

The Girl Who Never Made Mistakes by Mark Pett and Gary Rubinstein (Elementary Ages)

Beatrice Bottomwell is the star of this book and has never made a mistake, or so she thinks. The 9-year-old girl never forgets her math homework, never wears mismatched socks, and she always wins the

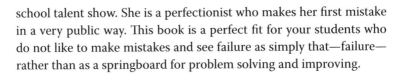
school talent show. She is a perfectionist who makes her first mistake in a very public way. This book is a perfect fit for your students who do not like to make mistakes and see failure as simply that—failure—rather than as a springboard for problem solving and improving.

Rosie Revere, Engineer by Andrea Beaty (Elementary Ages)

This is an illustrated story of a girl and her dream to become a great engineer. Rosie sees inspiration in things around her that others overlook. At night, in her room, she makes creations and inventions, including hot dog dispensers, helium pants, and python-repelling cheese hats. Her creations would surely impress if she would let anyone see them. Being afraid of failure, she hides her creations. During a visit from her Aunt Rose, she learns her creations are something to be celebrated.

Iggy Peck, Architect by Andrea Beaty (Elementary Ages)

The boy in this story is named Iggy, and he has one passion, which is architecture. He often uses surprising materials—much to his parents' delight and humor. Iggy has it easy until second grade, as his teacher does not like architecture. Iggy is banned from building at school until a field trip one day lets Iggy Peck show off his talents.

Mr. Ferris and His Wheel by Kathryn Gibbs Davis (Elementary Ages)

This illustrated picture book biography tells the story of how American inventor George Ferris defied gravity and difficult odds to invent the world's most iconic amusement park attraction, the Ferris wheel. Students are transported to the 1893 World's Fair.

Awesome Dawson by Chris Gall (Elementary Ages)

Dawson is the boy in this story, and his motto is that everything can be used again. He takes apart junk and uses the parts to make creations, from airplanes to fish tanks to robot friends. Dawson decides to make a robot that will do his chores for him. He does so, but the robot is a little too awesome and sucks up everything in sight. It destroys the town and frightens its residents. Dawson has to bring down his own creation and learns to use his creativity and skills to make life better for others, not just himself.

Going Places by Peter and Paul Reynolds (Elementary Ages)

In this book, a go-cart contest inspires kids' creativity to build a go-cart, race it, and win. Each kid grabs an identical kit, and hurries to build, with the exception of Maya. She is not in a hurry, and her go-cart is certainly unique. This book celebrates creativity, uniqueness, and thinking outside the box. This is a great reminder that not all projects should look alike.

Balloons Over Broadway: The True Story of the Puppeteer of Macy's Parade by Melissa Sweet (Elementary Ages)

In New York on Thanksgiving Day, giant new balloons will fill the skies for the Macy's Thanksgiving Day Parade. Students will be introduced to Tony Sarg, puppeteer extraordinaire. Using collage illustrations, the book tells the story of Sarg and his gift to America—helium balloons—which become the trademark of Macy's Parade.

What Do You Do With an Idea? by Kobi Yamada (Elementary Ages)

In this story, the child's confidence grows, and so does the idea. One day, something amazing happens. This is a story for all ages and for anyone who's ever had an idea that seems too big, too odd, and too difficult. After reading this book, students will be more open to allowing ideas they have to become a reality.

Book Ideas for Middle School and High School Students

- *The Big Book of Makerspace Projects: Inspiring Makers to Experiment, Create, and Learn* by Colleen Graves and Aaron Graves features many DIY, low-cost Makerspace projects.
- *The Invent to Learn Guide to Fun* by Josh Burker features classroom-tested maker projects.
- *62 Projects to Make With a Dead Computer (and Other Discarded Electronics)* by Randy Sarafan features more than 60 projects using discarded electronics combined with art.
- *The Art of Tinkering* by Karen Wilkinson and Mike Petrich celebrates tinkering, taking things apart, exploring, and building.
- *Maker Lab: 28 Super Cool Projects: Build, Invent, Create, and Discover* by Jack Challoner provides 28 kid-safe projects and crafts that will get young inventors thinking.

Tool-specific books are also available. An Amazon search for the specific tool you are using will locate appropriate books. A variety of these types of books would be an excellent student resource.

Keep Making

All activities that you do in your Makerspace will require that they be playful, purposeful, and planned. Playful is for student engagement. Purposeful and planned benefits everyone. We have to have a purpose for why we are doing what we are doing in our classrooms. If you plan with purpose in mind, you will easily be able to explain what you are doing and *why*.

Q: How much time do I need to devote to Makerspace each week or month?

A: As much as you can! Ideally, seeing kids at least weekly is best, but do what you can. Something is better than nothing!

February

Planning Pages and Reflections

Plan at least three thematic units that are purposeful, planned, and playful. You can use the challenge card ideas provided in this chapter or develop your own.

Unit #1 Broad Theme: _____

1. What will students be doing? How will it be planned, playful, and purposeful?

   _____
   _____
   _____

2. What materials will you need?

   _____
   _____
   _____

3. How and when will you implement this theme?

   _____
   _____
   _____

4. Any other notes for Unit #1?

   _____
   _____
   _____

Unit #2 Broad Theme: _____

1. What will students be doing? How will it be planned, playful, and purposeful?

   _____
   _____
   _____

Continues on next page . . .

2. What materials will you need?

_____

_____

_____

3. How and when will you implement this theme?

_____

_____

_____

4. Any other notes for Unit #2?

_____

_____

_____

Unit #3 Broad Theme: _____

1. What will students be doing? How will it be planned, playful, and purposeful?

_____

_____

_____

2. What materials will you need?

_____

_____

_____

3. How and when will you implement this theme?

_____

_____

_____

4. Any other notes for Unit #3?

_____

_____

_____

Continues on next page . . .

Select at least three books from the ideas provided in Chapter 7 or through your own research that will encourage creation, innovation, and problem solving. List the books you would like to use in class and why.

Book Title #1: _____

Why do you think it will promote, creativity, innovation, and/or problem solving?

_____
_____
_____
_____
_____

Book Title #2: _____

Why do you think it will promote, creativity, innovation, and/or problem solving?

_____
_____
_____
_____
_____

Book Title #3: _____

Why do you think it will promote, creativity, innovation, and/or problem solving?

_____
_____
_____
_____
_____

Structured Versus Unstructured Makerspaces in a Classroom, Schoolwide, or Districtwide Model

Success is no accident. It is hard work, perseverance, learning, studying, sacrifice and most of all, love of what you are doing or learning to do.

—Pelé

It always seems impossible until it is done.

—Nelson Mandela

MARCH TARGETS

- Identify the pros and cons of an unstructured Makerspace versus a structured Makerspace.
- Decide if you prefer a structured or unstructured Makerspace or a combination of the two.
- Plan your structured or unstructured Makerspace time.
- Determine times and days when students will come to structured (or unstructured) Makerspace time.
- Determine who will staff your Makerspace, where it will be, and when it will be open.
- Plan where students will store projects until they are complete and how you will assess each student.

Makerspaces vary greatly. No two are the same. What does a more structured Makerspace look like where classes visit on a regular schedule? I currently run a Makerspace where students come on a structured weekly basis. As I stated previously, students from grades 1–5 come once a week for 45 minutes. Kindergarten comes every other week for 30 minutes. I think students need a balance of open exploration as well as guided projects. This can be done with students coming at set times as well as having a Makerspace that kids come and go from.

Focusing on a Classroom, Schoolwide, or Districtwide Model

A classroom model is simple and flexible. Should you choose, you can have Makerspace time in your classroom when time permits and/or when the lesson you are teaching lends itself to a maker activity. It can also be a fun way to end the week. A Friday afternoon Makerspace time is always a hit with students. For a school- or districtwide model, you can achieve a successful Makerspace in a variety of ways. In my opinion, the best way to do this is to have a dedicated Makerspace teacher, classroom, and a set time that *every* student comes to the Makerspace. This ensures that each student is given equal opportunity for making. I realize this may not be feasible for many teachers or schools. Alternatively, you can have Makerspace days that all students participate in. These can be once a week or once a month, but ideally, students have the chance to make weekly. Classroom teachers can facilitate a weekly Makerspace in their classrooms. Districts and campuses can leave the planning up to each individual teacher or grade level, or enforce a more formal schedule. For example, one month, your entire campus or district can use Makerspace time to make cardboard creations, similar to Caine's Arcade (http://caines arcade.com). The next month, teachers might all use the Makerspace time for coding. What each classroom and grade level does will look different because of differing abilities and age groups, but, as always, the goal is the process, not the product.

At my school, we have hosted Makerspace Days. Some schools also call these STEAM Days or Innovation Days. You group students by combined grade levels (e.g., fourth and fifth grade together, and sixth and seventh grade together). The grouping is up to you and your campus. Each classroom teacher in each combined group plans a Makerspace activity. We had six teachers/classes per combined groups and limited rooms to 20 or fewer students. Students then look at the list of Makerspace activities and pick their top two choices of what interests them. Activities are added to a master list, and during Makerspace Day, each student goes to the room he or she has chosen and makes for a set amount of time. Table 5 outlines in more detail how this process is conducted at my school.

Structured Makerspaces

A structured Makerspace can go by other names, such as STEAM (or STEM) Lab or Innovation and Enrichment Lab, etc. The principle is the same. Students learn through a hands-on approach to making and working through the problem-solving process.

In my classroom, our Makerspace looks different from week to week. I like to keep a healthy balance between giving students challenges to solve, and giving them time to explore all of the amazing technology in our classroom, as well as pick from various rotations that interest them. We are structured, but within that structure students are given freedom of choice in technology rotations and how they go about solving problems. It's chaotic structure!

If you build a structured Makerspace, this will allow you to request material donations as needed. I would plan a rough outline of activities for each grading period. To begin, focus on the next grading period coming up at your school. Start from there, and plan challenges and activities for each group you will see. I will tell you from experience that if you teach all students in kindergarten through fifth grade, or all middle or high school students, you will go crazy having each grade level do a completely different activity. This is where differentiation is amazing because you can do very similar activities with grades K–2 and then grades 3–5. If you teach junior high or high school, I would group your grade levels into two clumps like I have done. You can vary the difficulty of the activity for the older classes.

Table 5

Makerspace Day Schedule, Instructions, and Activities

Mixed Grade Levels		
Grades K–1 8:15–9:00 (45 minutes) 16–17 students per room	Grades 2–3 8:45–9:45 (1 hour) 15–16 students per room	Grades 4–5 9:15–10:45 (1.5 hours) 16–17 students per room

- Each teacher will pick a Makerspace activity for his or her grouped grade levels.
- You will need to prepare and collect any needed materials. We will ask parents to volunteer to bring items, if needed, as well.
- If you need extra hands during your lesson, let me know. I will find volunteers.
- After you have chosen your activity, please record a brief summary of what it is on the master page.
- Students will pick their top two choices from the master list. After all students are assigned a room, a master list with student names will be sent to all teachers.
- After activities are complete, please line them up in the hallway against the walls. You can take your homeroom students on a gallery walk to see what everyone has made, at your convenience.

Master Activity List	
Young Explorers **(Grades K–1)**	Tracking Sea Turtles (Marine Biology) Pet Architecture (Architect) Animal Habitats and Camouflage (Wildlife Specialist) Dolphin Blubber (Marine Biology) Polar Bear Dens (Wildlife Specialist) Learning About Fossils (Paleontologist)
Junior Pioneers **(Grades 2–3)**	Creating Ice Cream (Food Scientist) Bubblegum Self-Portrait (Artists) Astronaut Food (Astronaut) Mixed Media Art (Artist) Theme Park Engineer (Engineer) Archaeological Dig (Archaeology)
Trailblazers **(Grades 4–5)**	Game Designer (Designer) Unconventional Art (Artist) Designing a Miniature Golf Course (Engineer) Designing a Windmill (Environmentalist) Wire Figures (Artist) Llama Mystery (Forensic Science)

Note. Lesson ideas are from Rozzy Learning Compacy, LLC, available at https://rozzylearningcompany.com.

Students *love* to repeat a challenge or activity.

When I first started, I tried to plan something different for each grade level. I quickly realized this was not practical. Again, I want this book to be practical and beneficial to you. You can learn from my mistakes. Initially, I thought that by planning separate activities and challenges for each grade level, the next year students would not "repeat" the same challenge. I made a huge error there. Students *love* to repeat a challenge or activity. Often I remind them we will do similar or the same challenges later in the year or next year, and they can already tell me what they will change, do differently, etc. That is reflection and redesigning at its finest. You can easily differentiate challenges by adding time constraints, measuring, limited use of materials, etc.

After you roughly plan out your challenges and activities, you can send a donation request list for each grading period. This will be helpful if you do not have a dedicated space for storage or know you won't be able to keep a massive amount of donations sorted. The following sections include examples of 6-week period challenge/activity outlines for three different grade bands, and a sample parent letter and donation request list you could use to accompany any of the outlines.

Sample Outline of Activities for Grades K–2 (for 6-Week Period)

- Marble runs
- Tinker stations
  - K'Nex challenges
  - LEGO challenges (structures/building/architecture around the world)
  - Magnets
  - Whatever you have on hand!

- Osmo Masterpiece
- Osmo Tangrams
- Three Little Pigs challenge
  - We will build our houses using LEGOs, magnetic blocks, KEVA planks, and straws with connectors, and the "Big Bad Wolf Blow Dryer" will try to blow our houses down!

- Tallest tower challenge
    - Design the tallest tower using variety of materials. Look at online pictures of how tall objects are built in our environment. Discuss attributes of each.
    - Materials for building towers: plastic cups, toilet paper and paper towel tubes, recycled plastic materials, LEGOs, magnetic blocks.

- Bridge challenge—Three Billy Goats Gruff
    - Toothpicks and marshmallows (will need six large marshmallows and 1/2-cup small marshmallows for each group, plus 50 toothpicks).
    - If we don't get marshmallows, we will use (backup plan) foam blocks, LEGOs, K'Nex, connector blocks, magnetic blocks, plastic blocks, or KEVA planks.

- Candy pumpkin towers challenge
    - Candy pumpkins work best; candy corn is too small for this age group to build with. (Trust me on this . . . I made this mistake!) Try to build a candy pumpkin tower using candy and toothpicks. Try to build it at least 12 inches tall. You must measure it!

- Doodle for Google Contest
    - Free contest; Google it.

Sample Outline of Activities for Grades 3–5 (for 6-Week Period)

- Marble runs with challenges, such as build a marble run that is at least 4 feet tall and has at least two 12-inch drops (pick what works for your group)!
- Tinker stations
    - K'Nex challenges
    - LEGO challenges (structures/building/architecture around the world)
    - Magnets
    - Whatever you have on hand!

- Tallest tower design
  - Use a variety of materials (e.g., spice drops and toothpicks, plastic cups, toilet paper and paper towel tubes, recycled plastic materials, LEGOs, magnetic blocks). From my experience, you will need three bags of spice drops for *each* class and 500 toothpicks for *each* class. Look at online pictures of how tall objects are built in our environment. Discuss attributes of each. Challenge by adding various perimeters.

- Chair design lesson
  - Challenge: Goldilocks needs your students' help. She broke Baby Bear's chair, and her mother insists that she make a new chair for him. Time for structural engineering! Students will use what they know about the strength of shapes and materials to design and build a chair that will hold the weight of a stuffed animal using only newspaper and tape.
  - Learning Objectives: After this activity, students should be able to: Describe and follow the steps of the engineering design process. Assess prototypes for strengths and weaknesses.
  - Challenge Notes:
    - Chair must be freestanding and on a flat surface.
    - You can rip or tear paper but no cutting.
    - Be creative; there is no right or wrong!
    - Is it okay if our chair collapses under the weight of the stuffed animal? Yes!
    - We can learn from our "mistakes"! Maybe you can add another leg to the chair or reinforce the seat.
    - Problem solve and work together!

- Marble maze with recycled materials (paper, tape, craft sticks, straws, marbles)
- Build a bridge that can hold up a Matchbox car and spans a 6-inch gap, or build a bridge for the Billy goats to cross past the mean old troll.
  - Toothpicks and marshmallows (will need six large marshmallows and 1/2-cup small marshmallows for each group, plus 50 toothpicks)
  - If we don't get marshmallows, we will use (backup plan) foam blocks, LEGOs, K'Nex, connector blocks, magnetic blocks, plastic blocks, or KEVA planks.

- Candy pumpkin towers
  - Candy pumpkins work best; candy corn is too small for this age group to build with. (*Note.* Trust me on this . . . I made this mistake!)
  - Try to build a candy pumpkin tower using candy and toothpicks. Try to build it at least 12 inches tall. You must measure it.

- Doodle for Google Contest
  - Free contest; Google it.

Sample Outline of Activities for Middle School and High School (for 6-Week Period)

- LEGO Robotics
- Coding
- Engineering and Math Area: Any activities given in the book or others you find (make your own marble mazes, tallest towers, bridge challenges)
- Art Area: Activities with literature connections, such as create something that represents a theme or character from a novel being studied or a unit of study
- Production Area: Details in Chapter 1
- Science: littleBits electrical snap circuits with challenge cards

Sample Donation Request Letter (for 6-Week Period)

Dear Parents and Community,

During the next 6 weeks in our Makerspace, we have some great science, technology, engineering, art, and math challenges and activities planned. In order to be able to offer these hands-on educational activities, we need your help. Below is a list of items we will need donated for this

6-week period. Thank you so much! (*Note.* You may want to include your rough outline of activities planned to help get parents/community on board and help them understand why you are requesting certain items.)

All the best,
Mrs. Brejcha

Big Items (to Borrow or Keep)

- Marble Run
- K'Nex
- LEGOs
- Magnets
- Marbles
- Matchbox cars (new or used)

Consumable Materials

- Spice drops
- Toothpicks
- Plastic cups
- Paper cups
- Toilet paper and paper towel tubes
- Recycled plastic materials (milk jugs, water bottles, etc.; cleaned out)
- Newspaper
- Tape (duct, masking, regular, any kind will work)
- Small stuffed animals (can be used)
- Paper (e.g., old greeting cards, construction or manila paper, any type of paper)
- Craft sticks (large and small)
- Straws
- Marshmallows (bags of large and small ones)
- Candy pumpkins

If Makerspace is new to your school, this might be an excellent way to ease into it. At this point, you will want to fully determine when your Makerspace time can fit into your week and decide on days and times with your team, district, and administration. Also start talking

about who will staff this area if you are forming a school- or districtwide model. If you are doing a classroom nook, this part will not be necessary. Many schools have a Makerspace in their library. This might be an option for your school. Brainstorm some ideas. There is no right or wrong.

If you are the only person on your campus offering this to your students, do it. You are an innovative forward thinker. Trust me, people will warm up to the idea. Give them a little time, and keep doing your thing. The students will love Makerspace and learn so many real-world skills. Students can help with adult buy-in because they love making and talking about it to adults around them.

Unstructured Makerspaces Sound Chaotic

An unstructured Makerspace requires a different mindset. For an unstructured Makerspace, students are given free rein to do and make with any material that is available. Each student does his or her own projects. It's not unusual for faculty to be timid about making in general to begin with, but you can certainly expect some chaos in an unstructured Makerspace. The plus is that you can control the chaos. If you decide to set your Makerspace up this way, I would suggest you start with a structured space and then transition to an unstructured Makerspace. The biggest factor to consider in this is the space and staffing. If your Makerspace is not structured with certain times students come and certain challenges they complete, your Makerspace will need to be open and staffed most of the day.

Unstructured Makerspace Times Within Structured Makerspace Time

I like to use unstructured Makerspace within our structured Makerspace time. At the end of each grading period, I provide a list of stations the students can visit. They choose where they go and how long they stay there. This might work well in your Makerspace all of the time. It really is a matter of preference, staffing, and space. I think a nice balance of structured and unstructured is ideal. I lean toward more structured time but certainly think a more unstructured approach is necessary at times. I would say in our Makerspace we do 70% structured and 30% unstructured during students' assigned time. It varies week to week.

It can be very beneficial for some students to work on projects for class during Makerspace time. This is a time when you can work alongside classroom teachers to piggyback on what they are teaching. Teachers can also assign open-ended projects for students to complete in the manner they choose during Makerspace. For example, an English language arts teacher could assign students a task to create something that represented a theme or character from a novel study they have completed or a favorite book.

Unstructured Makerspace Time

Lastly, you can create a totally unstructured Makerspace by providing materials and letting the students go. This will require a place for each student to store projects as they work so they can return to them the next time they come. This way can work, but it will be harder to identify standards students are learning as a whole. Documentation in this type of setting will likely require individual anecdotal records and reflection journaling from each student before students leave each day.

Excuse the laughter, chaos, volume, and mess . . . because students are learning! An unstructured space will be loud, fun, and messy—but controlled chaos. Expect that, and plan for it.

Providing a Student-Friendly, Organized Space

Keep in mind that whether structured or unstructured, you need to keep your Makerspace student-friendly. Students need defined work areas and easy access to materials. Create lots of places to display student work to help create a sense of ownership, to show students that what they created has value, and so others can see what is being done in Makerspace time. Make sure students know which items they

can use without permission and which items require permission to use. Items that would require permission should not be easily accessible. These would include materials such as hot glue guns, staple guns, any cutting instrument other than scissors, power tools, hand tools like a hammer, laser cutters, 3-D printers, and soldering irons—basically anything that you would not put out in a regular classroom. You can keep this simple by putting a printed out stop sign or red sticker dot on items that require permission to use.

Keep Making

> We learn by doing . . . brains are wired through hands-on interaction with the physical world.
> —Unknown

You do not have to have expensive technology and equipment. You can build in time for unstructured play and tinkering by opening your Makerspace at lunch and recess, and schedule time for students to bring their families to tinker in the space during an open house. Parents love to see a Makerspace in action. The concept makes more sense when you see what students are doing in the Makerspace.

The planning pages and reflections for this chapter will help you work through this decision. Be sure to take time to work carefully through each section so that you can lay the groundwork for your Makerspace to be successful. Remember there is no right or wrong answer. Do what feels like a natural extension to your curriculum and works best for your unique situation.

March

Planning Pages and Reflections

1. Plan staffing for structured Makerspace time. Who will teach it?

    _____

    _____

    _____

    _____

    _____

2. Where will your Makerspace be?

    _____

    _____

    _____

    _____

3. Determine times and days students will come to structured Makerspace time. When will Makerspace be taught within the week?

    _____

    _____

    _____

    _____

    You will want to do the following for each grading period if you are structuring your Makerspace in the manner listed above.

4. Plan a rough outline of activities and challenges for one grading period. See my sample for ideas (p. 125–129).

    _____

    _____

    _____

    _____

Continues on next page . . .

5. What donations will you need to ask for? List them here. See my sample for ideas.

   _____

   _____

   _____

   _____

   _____

6. For your unique situation and campus, list pros and cons for an unstructured space versus a structured Makerspace.

   _____

   _____

   _____

   _____

   _____

7. Talk with your team, administration, etc., and decide if an unstructured space will work for you. Decide if you prefer structured or unstructured, or a combination of the two, and why.

   _____

   _____

   _____

   _____

   _____

8. Plan your unstructured Makerspace times if you decide to go this route. Determine who will staff it, where it will be, and when it will be open.

   _____

   _____

   _____

   _____

   _____

Continues on next page . . .

9. Plan where students will store projects until they are complete and/or how you will assess each student individually or how they will record self-assessments and/or reflections.

    _____

    _____

    _____

    _____

    _____

10. When the Makerspace is open and unstructured, how does this look? How will you make sure students are meeting standards?

    _____

    _____

    _____

    _____

    _____

11. Talk with core subject teachers to see if they have ideas of ways students can create open-ended projects during scheduled Makerspace time that pertain to what they are covering in class. If you are a core subject teacher, what connections can you see happening in your classroom that can extend to Makerspace?

    _____

    _____

    _____

    _____

    _____

The Problem-Solving Process and Presentations of Projects and Challenges

Don't ask kids what they want to be when they grow up but what problems they want to solve. This changes the conversation from who do I want to work for, to what do I need to learn to be able to do that.

—Jaime Casap

APRIL TARGETS

- Display and be sure you are using the problem-solving process.
- Become proficient with each area of the process by giving examples of what each step looks like during a lesson.
- Plan and implement presentations of projects/challenges completed along with peer reviews.

Failure requires students to problem solve and rely on the problem-solving process, which I believe can help students problem solve in any situation, be it a real-world problem or a STEAM/Makerspace challenge. This is because failure can lead to success. Figure 36 features some quotes about failure that I have a poster of hanging in my classroom. It is an excellent reminder that failure means students should keep trying. It's okay to mess up.

You ideally will want to display the problem-solving process in all classrooms if you are approaching Makerspace as a schoolwide model. If you are using Makerspace as a grade-level model or similar format, you will want each classroom that has students come to Makerspace display the process. Your students can use it to solve a variety of problems. It should be the main visual they use as they work through challenges. The first poster is for the general education population (see Figure 2, p. 16). The second has been adapted for younger students who are not proficient readers and the students who are special education students on your campus or have modifications requiring picture anchors (see Figure 3, p. 16). It is great to go ahead and display both if you desire.

Q: What are some tips in dealing with projects that fail despite students' best efforts?

A: When using the problem-solving process, redesign is *expected*. Build a positive and trusting relationship with students first. They have to trust you to feel comfortable with failures . . . it's all about relationships you build.

The following sections include two lessons that follow the problem-solving process posters. I like to use my interactive whiteboard to show students how each part of the process is worked through:

- Yellow: Define the problem or challenge.
- Red: Plan solutions.
- Purple: Make a model or plan a strategy.
- Blue: Test the model or try it out.
- Green: Reflect and redesign.

We cannot solve our problems with the same level of thinking that created them. The measure of intelligence is the ability to change.

—Albert Einstein

I made 5,127 prototypes of my vacuum before I got it right. There were 5,126 failures. But I learned from each one. That's how I came up with a solution. So I don't mind failure.

—James Dyson

I'm an inventor. I became interested in long-term trends because an invention has to make sense in the world in which it is finished, not the world in which it is started.

—Ray Kurzweil

I have not failed, I've just found 10,000 ways that won't work.

—Thomas Edison

FIGURE 36. Quotes about failure.

Directions you give, if given on your projector or whiteboard, can be color-coded to match the process. It helps students make a visual connection between what they are working on and where they are at in the problem-solving process.

Challenge Example for Grades K—2

This challenge is a student favorite. My students ask for it over and over again. It is fun to do this one at the beginning of the school year (or whenever you're beginning your Makerspace) and again toward the end. Students become very clever along the way, and you can see the growth in their problem-solving skills.

Three Little Pigs Challenge (Combining Literature as Well!)

You will engineer houses from various materials, and the "Big Bad Wolf Hair Dryer" will try to blow your houses down.

Learning objectives/standard connections:
- **Science: Investigation and Experimentation:** Ask meaningful questions and conduct careful investigations.
- **Math:** Reason with shapes and their attributes and construct two- and three-dimensional shapes.

(*Teacher's Note.* The list could go on and on. It is super easy to weave in the standards you are expected to cover. Listen to your students as they work and write down what you hear; it's amazing.)

Let's walk through the problem-solving process using this activity. We began by watching a video of the "Three Little Pigs" story on the whiteboard. Then, I presented the challenge.

Define the Problem or Challenge: You need to engineer and build a house out of the materials provided that the "Big Bad Wolf Hair Dryer" cannot blow down. You must keep your pig safe. (*Teacher's Note.* Use any materials you have for building. I used harder materials like straws and paper for older students and a variety of blocks for younger students. I told them when the visual timer went off, the wolf would be coming to try and blow down their house. For pigs, you can use paper cutouts or plastic little pigs. They were so excited to get started.)

Plan Solutions: Work with your team using the dry erase tables or paper, and make plans for building houses out of the various materials provided. (*Teacher's Note.* See Figure 37.)

Make a Model: Let students use their planning and make a house. (*Teacher's Note.* Students will build houses and ensure their plastic pig is safely inside; see Figure 38.)

Test Your Model: The "Big Bad Wolf Hair Dryer" will come and try to blow your house down! (*Teacher's Note.* To test this particular challenge, I came around with the "Big Bad Wolf Hair Dryer" and tried to blow their houses down; see Figure 39.)

Reflect and Redesign: If your house stood up to the "Big Bad Wolf," why do you think it did? If not, what do you need to change? (*Teacher's Note.* Give students the opportunity to try again if their building failed. I also told them to continue thinking about ways to redesign, and we repeated this activity about 12 weeks later.)

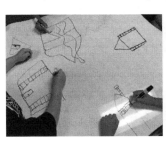

FIGURE 37. Students planning the Three Little Pigs Challenge.

FIGURE 38. Students building models for the Three Little Pigs Challenge.

FIGURE 39. The "big bad wolf hair dryer" in action.

Challenge Example for Grades 3—5

For this challenge, we reviewed the story "Goldilocks and the Three Bears," and students were presented with a challenge to make Baby Bear a new chair.

Goldilocks and the Three Bears— Chair Design Lesson

You will make Baby Bear a new chair.

Standards Connections/Learning Objectives: After this activity, you should be able to describe and follow the steps of the problem-solving process and assess prototypes for strengths and weaknesses.

Define the Challenge: Goldilocks needs your help! She broke Baby Bear's chair, and her mother insists that she make a new chair for him. Time for structural engineering.

Plan Solutions: Use what you know about the strength of shapes and materials to plan a design to build a chair that will hold the weight of a stuffed animal using only newspaper and tape.

Make a Model:
- Use only the supplies provided to build a chair that will support your stuffed animal (paper and tape).
- The chair must be freestanding and on a flat surface.
- You can rip or tear paper, but no cutting.
- Be creative—there is no right or wrong.

Test Your Model: Is it okay if our chair collapses under the weight of the stuffed animal? Yes!

Reflect and Redesign: We can learn from our "mistakes." Maybe you can add another leg to the chair or reinforce the seat.

Students reflected and redesigned as they worked to make a successful model by problem solving and working together. Figure 40 includes some photos of students working on this challenge. Middle school and high school students should be able to follow the problem-solving process more independently. Make sure that the process is displayed and that you talk about it often.

When Group Work Doesn't Work

Often when students work in groups, they don't agree on the best solution to solve the problem. When this happens, I typically give students a little while to try to work it out. They usually do. If they can't move forward, I will meet with the group members and help them converse and share their ideas, and then facilitate them in working together, including aspects of each student's ideas from the planning stage.

Presentations of Projects and/or Challenges

Students create models and plan strategies every day they are in a Makerspace. Making is essentially creating a model to test and then redesigning if needed. If you use the problem-solving process presented in this book, Step #3 is: Make a model or plan a strategy.

Make it clear that students will be respectful of each other while making and during peer reviews . . . period.

Creativity to this extent requires students to take risks as they work on projects and share them with their peers. As I've said, remind them often that it's okay to fail, and it's okay to not be right or not have the right answer. Working in a Makerspace is about messing up, trying again, and again, and again, and working through problems using the problem-solving process with their peer group. Make it clear that students will be respectful of each other while making and during peer reviews . . . period. It's not an option; it's just how it is.

Students can share in a variety of ways, ranging from simply verbally sharing what they are learning and trying with their group, to actually presenting what they have done. This can be done using apps for presentations, such as Vidra, PowToon, Storyboard, Prezi, iMovie, etc. The list is virtually endless and will change as technology and resources change. This is a great opportunity to lay down the basics of

FIGURE 40. Students working on the chair design challenge.

what you want presented and conveyed to the group and then let your students choose the method of delivery. This provides choice while still holding students accountable. Figure 41 includes some photos of students working on presentations and presenting their work. My students like to share and present their projects mostly with technology. They love using the Apple TV to AirPlay the presentation they have made for the entire class to see and hear. I have also had students use our poster maker machine to make a poster using Canva and then print it large enough for everyone to see. Some students prefer to simply speak to the class and show what they have done. There is really no right or wrong here.

Peer Reviews and the TAG Method

For peer reviews, I like to keep it pretty simple and positive using the TAG method. I do not remember where I learned this. It was not my idea, but it's awesome and easy:

- **T**ell something you liked.
- **A**sk a question.
- **G**ive a positive suggestion.

That's it. It's very easy to remember and causes students to give feedback to others in a positive way. You may already have a peer review policy or practice you use; if so, keep using that if it works

Preparation to present: Presentation ideas:

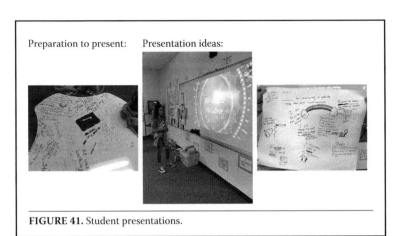

FIGURE 41. Student presentations.

for you. The main focus is on positive feedback and asking reflective questions. Students have to feel comfortable with you and their peers for this to work.

Keep Making—and Remember Creativity

For a Makerspace or classroom to be successful, it must have creativity. Creativity is not just being a good artist—creativity is innovation. You will find that having your students create models, give presentations, and conduct peer reviews will really allow their creativity to shine. This type of learning makes it clear to students that everything is not black and white; there is not always one right answer. This is hard for students to grasp at first. They are so used to an answer being right or wrong that your higher achieving students, especially, will struggle at first. They strive to be right, and when there is little black and white and lots of grey area, that can stump them sometimes. Working in a Makerspace is real-life learning that requires innovation and creativity. Plus, it's fun. It also requires a fair amount of vulnerability from students because peers will review each other and offer feedback.

Sometimes the craziest ideas turn out to be great. When students make models and presentations of their work, they will improvise as they work. What they had planned may not work and they will have to regroup, reflect, and redesign.

April

Planning Pages and Reflections

1. What is your plan for displaying and using the problem-solving process? Which classrooms will utilize the process and why? Where will you display it so it is easily seen by all students and can become common language on your campus or for your grade level, etc.?

   _____

   _____

   _____

   _____

   _____

2. Give examples for each step using a challenge you would like to implement soon. How will each step of the problem-solving process look in your classroom during your lesson?
   - Step #1: Define the problem or challenge. What might this look like?

     _____

     _____

     _____

     _____

     _____

   - Step #2: Plan solutions. What might this look like?

     _____

     _____

     _____

     _____

     _____

Continues on next page . . .

- Step #3: Make a model or plan a strategy. What might this look like?

  _____
  _____
  _____
  _____
  _____

- Step #4: Test the model or try it out. What might this look like?

  _____
  _____
  _____
  _____
  _____

- Step #5: Reflect and redesign. What might this look like?

  _____
  _____
  _____
  _____
  _____

3. How will students present and share their projects with others?

   _____
   _____
   _____
   _____
   _____

4. How will peer reviews work in your Makerspace?

   _____
   _____
   _____
   _____
   _____

Technology Integration and High(er) Tech Materials

Technology is permeating every single thing we do . . . And to the extent that we can better expose our young people to all the different ways that technology can be used, not just for video games or toys, we're planning for the future.

—Marc Morial

Good, bad or indifferent, if you are not investing in new technology, you are going to be left behind.

—Philip Green

MAY TARGETS

- Give examples of meaningful technology integration for your Makerspace. How can you acquire desired high-tech devices and programs?
- Plan how you will implement these in your Makerspace.
- Determine who is responsible for charging devices, updating devices, fixing broken items, resetting passwords, etc.

Computer literacy is now an expected component in education. Demand for computer engineers, system administrators, technology coordinators, and other STEAM professions continues to rise. You can integrate meaningful technology into Makerspaces in so many ways. In this chapter, I have just a few ideas of items that you may want to consider adding to your Makerspace. I have purposely saved this chapter for last because this area seems to cause teachers the most pause. Because you have successfully implemented so many wonderful making activities so far, I hope this chapter will inspire you to spend this month and the months ahead thinking of ways you can add even more to your Makerspace.

Considerations Before You Start Using Higher Tech Materials

The suggestions in this chapter are not necessary to run an amazing Makerspace. If you don't have access to devices and apps, don't worry about it. Do think of ways you can acquire some higher tech items, such as through grants, budgeting for next school year, etc. Again, these are "bonus" items. You can have a great Makerspace without these items. I do suggest your goal should be to add lots of meaningful technology as you are able to, but I do not want to see you without a Makerspace because you do not have these items. You can inspire students to create, make, innovate, and tinker while problem solving without any of these items. Process over product, once again.

You do *not* have to know how to do it all.

The most important advice I can give in regards to technology is that you do *not* have to know how to do it all. Your students will most likely learn much faster than you. When you get something new, get it out and ask them to help you figure it out together. You will be shocked at what they already know and how naturally certain skills come to certain students. It's amazing, truly, to see what their inher-

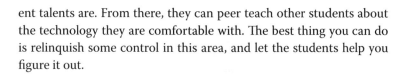

ent talents are. From there, they can peer teach other students about the technology they are comfortable with. The best thing you can do is relinquish some control in this area, and let the students help you figure it out.

Taking Care of Devices

When you allow students to use higher priced materials, it's imperative that they know how to use them appropriately. Lay out very clear expectations for use, and note that if they do not follow your expectations, they may lose the privilege of using the material for that class time. If you have to take away a material be sure they understand what specific action or behavior they were doing that is not appropriate. Be willing to extend some extra grace initially. They will be *very* excited and eager to get their hands on new objects. That's just the nature of students.

Daily Charging of Devices and Cord Management

The downside to technology is that it will require someone to be in charge of charging daily. All of the products in this chapter have to be charged before using. Unfortunately, they do not all take the same power cord. You will need someone who can manage the cords and make sure items are charged daily and ready for students to use. This takes more time than you might think.

I charge items in buckets that also house the cords that go with each item (see Figure 42). Lots of items, like Dash and Dot robots and Bee-Bots, will roll off counters if they are not contained. I have a lock-and-charge cart for Chromebooks and iPads. Find what works for you. Cord management is always an issue to some extend (at least for me).

Building a Deconstruction Station

One great idea if you have access to older technology that is broken and is going to be trashed is to have a deconstruction station. Often, parents and community members are happy to donate their old

FIGURE 42. Charging and cord management of devices.

electronics to you. At this station, it's as simple and fun as it sounds. Students disassemble and investigate as they deconstruct. They learn so much about electronics, computers, circuits, etc., in general while doing this. You will need old electronics and basic tools, such as a variety of screwdrivers, a hammer, a hex key set, etc. You can take this station a step further and have students try to create something new out of what has been taken apart. Figure 43 includes a picture of a simple deconstruction station and a sample note of what I sent home over the Remind app and in our school newsletter to inform parents.

Technology Integration Ideas

littleBits

littleBits are easy-to-use electronic building blocks that empower students to invent (littleBits Electronics Inc., 2011–2018). The blocks are color-coded, magnetic, and reusable. The kits are fun and allow students to be infinitely creative (see Figure 44). They are also a wonderful way to expose children and young adults to electrical snap circuits. The color-coded bits mean that students quickly learn after being taught that the blue bits are for power, pink bits are for input, green bits are for output, and orange is for wires. You can have stu-

A new station in Makerspace this year will be a deconstruction station! At this station, it's as simple and fun as it sounds. Students disassemble and investigate as they deconstruct. They learn about electronics, computers, circuits, etc., as they take electronics apart. We will need old electronics as donations and basic tools, such as a variety of screwdrivers, hex key sets, etc. If you label donated broken electronics with your child's name and homeroom teacher, I will make sure your child gets to take that item apart in his or her group. Students will also try to create something new out of what has been taken apart. Thank you!

FIGURE 43. Sample deconstruction station and parent letter.

FIGURE 44. Students using littleBits.

dents create simple circuits that have timers, make a little fan blow, or make a horn sound—the list is endless. After having taught a Makerspace for a year, I realized we went through 9-volt batteries very fast using littleBits. You need to budget or plan for buying 9-volt batteries. littleBits lend themselves well to a discussion on open and closed circuits. This is a specific learning object typically introduced around grade 4.

Snap Circuits Junior

I like Snap Circuits Junior kits for younger grades, especially younger elementary students. The kit is simple due to the colorful pictures and challenges included, and it allows students to create their own electronics and experiments (see Figure 45). All projects are made on a plastic grid, which is something that sets these apart from littleBits in terms of being more user-friendly for younger kids. You will need two AA batteries for each kit along with new batteries as needed. Snap Circuits, much like littleBits, also are a great way to introduce and further explore open and closed electrical circuits.

Osmo: Monster, Masterpiece, Tangram, Newton, Coding, and More

I encourage you to visit the Osmo website at https://www.play osmo.com. Osmo has an amazing assortment of great apps for iOS with hands-on tangible play pieces. You won't be disappointed. Osmo is continually looking for new ways to add to the Osmo collection. We use Osmo almost daily because of the variety of apps it offers (see Figure 46). Younger students love Osmo Monster (https://www. playosmo.com/en/monster/). Mo is the monster, who leads the kids through different stories, and he asks the kids to draw pictures of items needed for the story. After each drawing, he picks up what the student has drawn on his or her white creative board and pulls it onto the screen to use as part of the interactive story. You will need to plan and budget for extra dry erase markers for your creative boards. The creative boards do come with some dry erase markers, but they will not last very long with continued use.

Osmo Masterpiece (https://www.playosmo.com/en/masterpiece/) combines technology and pencil-and-paper drawing for interactive drawing. Osmo Tangram (https://www.playosmo.com/en/tangram/) is great for math skills, visual problem solving, and spatial skills. Student use hands-on tangible puzzle pieces to play. Osmo Newton (https://www.playosmo.com/en/newton/) combines physics and problem solving. Students use inventive objects, such as hand-drawn pictures or anything around them, to guide falling on-screen balls into targeted zones. Osmo has new apps with tangible play coming out

FIGURE 45. Using Snap Circuits Junior.

FIGURE 46. Students using Osmo.

fairly regularly. Two of the newest items are Osmo Coding and Osmo Hot Wheels MindRacers. Remember that iPads will always need to be charged.

Bee-Bot Programmable Floor Robot

Bee-Bot is a programmable floor robot designed for use by young children. It's easy to operate and ideal for teaching sequencing, estimation, problem solving, and more (Terrapin Software, 2016). Using the robot, students can enter up to 40 commands, which send Bee-Bot forward, back, left, and right. Bee-Bots are a great way to introduce basic

coding. My students in grades K–5 all enjoy using them. Depending on which grade level I see, what we do with them varies. The younger students simply enjoy programming them. Older students will enjoy a challenge, such as programing the Bee-Bot through an obstacle course or using a large floor track to draw a course and then program their robot to follow the course. Keep in mind that Bee-Bots also need to be regularly charged.

You can also make your own Bee-Bot floor mats to integrate coding with a skill being taught in your classroom. Mats can be made to help students learn shapes, colors, sight words, reading words, spelling words, numbers, etc. You can introduce task cards to challenge students to get their Bee-Bot from one spot on the board to the other (see Figure 47). Each square needs to be 15 cm. That is the distance the Bee-Bot moves for each individual input given. You can download free printable Bee-Bot shape mat and challenge cards on Tes at https://www.tes.com/teaching-resource/bee-bot-shape-mat-and-challenge-cards-11009699. For a small fee, you can also download this printable mat, which is perfect for a unit about colors, on Teachers Pay Teachers at https://www.teacherspayteachers.com/Product/BEE-BOT-Colors-2701378.

Quiver Augmented Reality

Quiver Education is an augmented reality coloring app. Essentially, it uses 3-D augmented reality to bring coloring pages to life for students. Quiver has many options to meet your needs. It has basic pages students can color and then scan using the Quiver app to develop a 3-D model. It really is lots of fun. In Quiver's educational packs, you can find pages that focus on educational content, and Quiver Fashion allows your students to create fashion designs and then bring them to life. You will need to print a copy of each page used for each student and provide crayons (see Figure 48). If you have Apple TV in your classroom, let students each come up and show their 3-D creations using AirPlay. iPads will have to be charged regularly. (Notice the pattern here—charging will take time and forethought for using many of the apps and devices suggested in this chapter.)

FIGURE 47. Students using Bee-Bots.

FIGURE 48. Students coloring with Quiver.

Hour of Code

Hour of Code provides one-hour coding courses that are available in more than 45 languages. The best part is: No experience is needed from you or your students. There are fun activities for students of all ages, created by a variety of partners and for a variety of subjects. If you have never done Hour of Code, it sounds very intimidating. I promise you, it is one of the easiest lessons you will teach because Hour of Code makes it easy for each student to pick areas that interest him or her, and the online tutorials walk students through each step. In order to complete a full hour-long tutorial, we spend two class sessions on Hour of Code. I introduce it in detail and explain why it

is valuable. I also let students know that each student who completes the full hour will receive an Hour of Code Certificate. If you don't have enough devices for each student, please still visit Hour of Code and look for its section on "unplugged" coding. Students can still earn an Hour of Code Certificate for doing unplugged activities. I provide a QR code for my students to scan that takes them directly to the Hour of Code kids section so they can get started quickly. iPads, tablets, and/or laptops or Chromebooks will need to be charged regularly. Figure 49 is an example of the poster hanging in my room. You will also find certificates of completion and more promotional and reward ideas on the Hour of Code website.

Dash and Dot Robots

Dash and Dot robots are ready to go right out of the box and are pretty durable. They interact with students, their environment, and each other with built-in motors, sensors, LEDs and audio abilities. Students engage in critical thinking, creativity, communication, and collaboration. These robots are an easy way to introduce students to computer science and coding.

I only have three Dash robots and one Dot. I include them in a station that students have to rotate through, and when it is their turn, they are beyond excited (see Figure 50). There are so many coding activities you can do with Dash and Dot. You will have to keep these devices charged as well. You can even combine Dash and Dot robots with other devices, like littleBits. Figure 51 shows an exciting competition we had to see who could knock down the wooden blocks first.

Cubelets Modular Robots

Cubelets Robot Blocks make it easy for students to learn how to use modular robots. These little cubes are really cool. Each one has a different function. Cubelets come with a direction and description card for each cube (see Figure 52). I took the description cards out right away, hole punched them, and put them on a ring so they would not get lost and so students could reference them easily. You will have to keep the power cube charged.

HOUR
OF
CODE

IPADS: Select QR reader & scan code

Desktop or Chromebook:
Go to the website
https://hourofcode.com/us/learn

FIGURE 49. Hour of Code classroom poster.

FIGURE 50. Students working with Dash and Dot robots.

FIGURE 51. Students using Dash and Dot robots with littleBits and blocks.

FIGURE 52. Students working with Cubelets.

Bloxels

For your students who love video games and seem obsessed with them, Bloxels is a great alternative. Students build their own video games on the Bloxel game board using tiny cubes that have different functions according to their colors to create a game that can be uploaded into the app after creation. Students can actually play the game they made. This activity seems to be a love or hate one. Most of my students feel strongly about it one way or the other.

Ollie and Sphero

Ollie and Sphero are app-enabled robots (see Figure 53). Sphero is a spherical robot capable of rolling around and is controlled by a smartphone or tablet. Ollie is a leader in robots for speed and stunts. Ollie is fast and fun and operates on a variety of tracks and turf. These are very durable robots.

Arduino

Arduino is an open-source electronic platform that enables users to create interactive electronic objects. These are fun little kits that initially appear very tricky, but students figure them out very quickly (see Figure 54).

Other Ideas

Tablets Loaded With Production and Research Apps

This list is far from exhaustive, and new apps come out all of the time. Try and stay current by researching new apps often.
- 30hands
  - http://30hands.com
  - This app is a digital storytelling tool that helps students tell stories, explain a concept, or teach others with fast and easy video creation.

FIGURE 53. Students working with Ollie and Sphero.

FIGURE 54. A student working with Arduino.

- ♦ Book Creator
  - – https://bookcreator.com
  - – This app allows students to combine text, images, audio, and video to create interactive stories, digital portfolios, research journals, poetry books, science reports, instruction manuals, comics, and more.

- ♦ Canva
  - – https://www.canva.com
  - – This photo editor and graphic design app is my favorite.

161

- ChatterPix Kids
  - http://www.duckduckmoose.com/educational-iphone-itouch-apps-for-kids/chatterpixkids
  - This app lets students add a mouth and voice to any picture.

- Daisy the Dinosaur
  - http://www.daisythedinosaur.com
  - This free app introduces basic coding for ages 5–7.

- DOGOnews
  - https://www.dogonews.com
  - This website, which also has an app, features fun articles for kids on current events, science, sports, and more.

- Doodle Buddy
  - https://itunes.apple.com/us/app/doodle-buddy-paint-draw-scribble-sketch-its-addictive/id313232441?mt=8
  - This app allows students to paint, draw, scribble, and sketch.

- Dot and Dash apps
  - https://www.makewonder.com/apps
  - There's a series of programming and coding apps that pair with Dash and Dot robots.

- Epic!
  - https://www.getepic.com/educators
  - This digital library app provides unlimited children's books.

- Do Ink
  - http://www.doink.com
  - This app makes it easy to create incredible green screen videos and photos.

- Hopscotch
  - https://www.gethopscotch.com
  - Students can learn to code and make their own games.

- Kiddle
  - https://www.kiddle.co
  - Kiddle is a visual search engine for kids.

- Kodable
  - https://www.kodable.com
  - Kodable is an easy-to-use app that teaches programming for kids.

- LEGO Movie Maker
  - https://itunes.apple.com/us/app/lego-movie-maker/id516001587?mt=8
  - Kids can create stop motion movies with this free app from LEGO.

- Lightbot: Code Hour
  - http://lightbot.com/hour-of-code.html
  - This is a free coding and programming adventure game for students of any grade level.

- Ollie
  - https://www.sphero.com/ollie
  - Ollie is an app-controlled robot. The free app allows students to control and experiment with Ollie's speed, acceleration, turn radius, and lights.

- Osmo
  - https://www.playosmo.com
  - There are several apps and accessories for use with the Osmo iPad base.

- Photo Booth
  - https://support.apple.com/guide/photo-booth/welcome/mac
  - Students can use the Photo Booth app on MacOS or similar iOS or Android apps, like Simple Booth or LumaBooth, to develop their own photo booths.

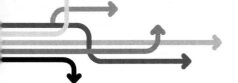

- Pic Stitch
  - https://bigblueclip.com/portfolio/pic-stitch
  - Students can easily make photo collages with this free app.

- Scratch Jr.
  - https://www.scratchjr.org
  - This free app introduces a programming language that enables young children (ages 5–7) to create their own interactive stories and games.

- Sphero app
  - https://edu.sphero.com/d
  - This free app operates Sphero robots.

- Stop Motion Studio
  - https://www.cateater.com
  - This app features easy stop-motion moving-making for students.

- Tickle
  - https://tickleapp.com
  - This easy-to-learn programming and coding app allows students to work with and program a variety of robots and other smart devices from one interface.

- Tynker
  - https://www.tynker.com/mobile
  - Tynker is a complete system that teaches kids to code.

- Wonderopolis
  - https://wonderopolis.org
  - This is a great site for kids to explore their wonders and add to your wonder wall.

LEGO Robotics

LEGO Robotics are huge on many campuses. My goal is to lay a good foundation at the elementary campus in all of the prerequisites required to code, engineer, problem solve, create, make a model, reflect, and redesign so that when they get to middle school and high school, students are ready to jump right into the LEGO Robotics program. We do have a LEGO Robotics kit that we use and work with. There are so many options when it comes to LEGO Robotics. You will have to do some research and decide what your district or campus believes is attainable and relevant. You can start by searching online for "LEGO Robotics" or visiting: http://www.legoengineering.com/general-advice-for-getting-started.

Green Screen

Weather forecasts and many television shows and movies utilize a tool called a *green screen*. A green screen is a solid-colored background used behind the subject of a photo or video that allows filmmakers to replace the solid backdrop with a new background. All you need is a device with an appropriate app and a green screen (or green curtain). Remember to keep those devices charged.

3-D Printer

If you are fortunate enough to have access to a 3-D printer, you will find many websites useful in creating 3-D print files. Many 3-D printers come with curriculum for teachers to use in the classroom or that you can use in your Makerspace. If you do not have a 3-D printer, you can also use the sites below to introduce your students to 3-D design. Even if they cannot print their designs, students can create 3-D print files.

My go-to is Tinkercad (https://www.tinkercad.com), which is a free online 3-D design and printing app. Students can start by working on beginner tutorials and then begin working through quests under the "learn" tab. For ideas, inspirations, and access to a community of learners, you can also visit its blog at: https://blog.tinkercad.com. Even if you don't have a 3-D printer, you can still use this free program to introduce students to 3-D design. One other app that is worth looking into is SketchUp. You can learn more at https://i.materialise.com/blog/first-3d-model-in-sketchup-tutorial and https://www.sketchup.com.

Keep Making

Education is the most powerful weapon which you can use to change the world.

—Nelson Mandela

Again, I encourage you to just start making with your students. I love the idea of structuring a Makerspace around students visiting five different stations, one for each area of STEAM. For example, if you have limited Bee-Bots, Dash and Dot robots, Osmo kits, littleBits, and/or a LEGO Wall, you can build your stations around STEAM:

- Science: littleBits or Snap Circuits (Junior or Regular)
- Technology: Bee-Bots, Dash and Dot, etc.
- Engineering: LEGO wall with specific challenges
- Art: Make It Station
- Math: Osmo Tangram

Remember that the ideas listed in this chapter are not necessary; they are a bonus. So often students are more excited to make things out of recycled materials than they are about technology. Do what works for your students. You can keep your Makerspace as simple as a nook with an activity or rotations for each area of STEAM. If you are short on high(er) tech materials, do rotations so all students get a turn.

May

Planning Page and Reflections

1. Give examples of meaningful technology integration for your Makerspace that you see as relevant for your unique situation.

   _____

   _____

   _____

   _____

   _____

2. How can you acquire desired high(er) tech devices and programs?

   _____

   _____

   _____

   _____

   _____

3. Plan how you will implement higher tech in your Makerspace.

   _____

   _____

   _____

   _____

   _____

4. Who is responsible for charging devices, updating devices, fixing broken items, resetting passwords, etc.? (Trust me, this will take time out of someone's day.)

   _____

   _____

   _____

   _____

   _____

CONCLUSION

Keep Making

Building a Makerspace can be this simple: Just start making. We have to do this for our students. Regardless of whether today's students work in technical careers, become doctors or politicians, or whatever they choose, we know that with the challenges their generation will face, they will be expected to be problem solvers who are educated in science, technology, engineering, art, and math and have excellent soft skills. STEAM is gaining attention in government and research as well. With global competition rising, America must rethink its economic future. Makerspaces and STEAM education are opportunities for our students to be the innovators, creators, and technical leaders of the world. This is a pivotal point for Americans, and it must begin at the elementary level and continue through high school.

If it's good for students, it's the right thing to do.

Thank you for joining me and allowing me to be a part of creating and maintaining your Makerspace. If it's good for students, it's the right thing to do. Makerspaces are beyond good for all students. Have fun, and I would love to hear about how you are implementing the ideas presented in this book and integrating your own ideas as well. Visit my website at http://makerspacesinschool.com to get in touch. Makerspaces grow, evolve, and change over the years, making us all lifelong learners. Start making and don't stop.

References

ATTN. (2017). *Mike Rowe on Hollywood's portrayal of blue-collar workers* [Video]. Retrieved from https://www.attn.com/stories/18803/mike-rowe-hollywoods-portrayal-blue-collar-workers

Community for Advancing Discovery Research in Education. (2014). *Improving STEM curriculum and instruction: Engaging students and raising standards* [STEM Smart Brief]. Waltham, MA: Education Development Center. Retrieved from http://successfulstemeducation.org/resources/improving-stem-curriculum-and-instruction-engaging-students-and-raising-standards

Cooper, J. (2013). Designing a school makerspace. *Edutopia*. Retrieved from https://www.edutopia.org/blog/designing-a-school-makerspace-jennifer-cooper

Desilver, D. (2017). *U.S. students' academic achievement still lags that of their peers in many other countries.* Retrieved from http://www.pewresearch.org/fact-tank/2017/02/15/u-s-students-internationally-math-science

Families.com. (n.d.) *Anxious? Depressed? Get that right brain working* [Web log post]. Retrieved from https://www.families.com/blog/anxious-depressed-get-that-right-brain-working

Fayer, S., Lacey, A., & Watson, A. (2017). STEM occupations: Past, present, and future. *Spotlight on Statistics.* Retrieved from https://www.bls.gov/spotlight/2017/science-technology-engineering-and-mathematics-stem-occupations-past-present-and-future/home.htm

Hamilton, B. J. (2015). *Makerspaces, participatory learning, and libraries* [Web log post]. Retrieved from https://theunquietlibrarian.wordpress.com/2012/06/28/makerspaces-participatory-learning-and-libraries

Harris Interactive, & Microsoft Corp. (2011). *STEM perceptions: Student & parent study.* Retrieved from https://news.microsoft.com/download/archived/presskits/citizenship/docs/STEMPerceptionsReport.pdf

Hill, J. (2017). *STEM education grows interest in NDT field as a career* [Web log post]. Retrieved from http://www.spacescienceservices. com/new-blog/2017/1/11/stem-education-grows-interest-in-ndt-field-as-a-career

Khan, I. (2015). *Technology growing at an unprecedented rate* [Web log post]. Retrieved from http://www.solgenia.com/blog/technology-growing-at-an-unprecedented-rate

Kroeger, J. (2016). *Importance of STEM education in elementary school.* Retrieved from https://education.fsu.edu/importance-stem-education-elementary-school

Langdon, D., McKittrick, G., Beede, D., Khan, B., & Doms, M. (2011). *STEM: Good jobs now and for the future* [ESA Issue Brief #03-11]. Washington, DC: U.S. Department of Commerce Economics and Statistics Administration. Retrieved from http://www.esa.doc. gov/reports/stem-good-jobs-now-and-future

littleBits Electronics Inc. (2011–2018). *littleBits.* Retrieved from https://littlebits.cc

McClure, E. R., Guernsey, L., Clements, D. H., Bales, S. N., Nichols, J., Kendall-Taylor, N., & Levine, M. H. (2017). *STEM starts early: Grounding science, technology, engineering and math education in early childhood.* New York, NY: The Joan Ganz Cooney Center at Sesame Workshop. Retrieved from http://joanganzcooneycenter. org/publication/stem-starts-early

National Science Foundation. (2013). *Inspiring STEM learning: Education and & human resources* [NSF 13-800]. Arlington, VA: Author. Retrieved from https://www.nsf.gov/about/congress/reports/ehr_research.pdf

Nepris. (2013–2018). *Connecting industry to every classroom.* Retrieved from https://www.nepris.com/foreducators

Noonan, R. (2017). *STEM jobs: 2017 update* [ESA Issue Brief #02-17]. Washington, DC: U.S. Department of Commerce Economics and Statistics Administration. Retrieved from http://www.esa. doc.gov/reports/stem-jobs-2017-update

Preble, L. (n.d.). Teachers must encourage student creativity. *TeachHUB.* Retrieved from http://www.teachhub.com/teaching-creativity

Robinson, K. (2006). *Do schools kill creativity?* [Video]. Retrieved from https://www.ted.com/talks/ken_robinson_says_schools_kill_creativity

Terrapin Software. (2016). *Bee-Bot.* Retrieved from https://www. bee-bot.us

Thinkers & Tinkers. (2014). *What is the maker movement?* Retrieved from http://hernbergm.wixsite.com/maker-movement/background

U.S. Bureau of Labor Statistics. (2013). *Occupational employment projects to 2022.* Retrieved from https://www.bls.gov/opub/mlr/2013/ article/occupational-employment-projections-to-2022.htm

U.S. News & World Report. (2014). *U.S. News & World Report unveils the U.S. News/Raytheon STEM Index.* Retrieved from https://www.usnews.com/info/blogs/press-room/2014/04/23/ us-news-unveils-the-us-news-raytheon-stem-index

Vilorio, D. (2014, Spring). STEM 101: Intro to tomorrow's jobs. *Occupational Outlook Quarterly.* Retrieved from https://www. bls.gov/careeroutlook/2014/spring/art01.pdf

White, R. E. (2015). *The power of play: A research summary on play and learning.* St. Paul, MN: Minnesota Children's Museum. Retrieved from https://mcm.org/wp-content/uploads/2015/09/ MCMResearchSummary1.pdf

Wikipedia. (2018). *Soft skills.* Retrieved from https://en.wikipedia. org/wiki/Soft_skills

World Economic Forum. (2016). *The future of jobs: Employment, skills and workforce strategy for the fourth industrial revolution.* Geneva, Switzerland: Author. Retrieved from http://reports. weforum.org/future-of-jobs-2016

Additional Resources

Websites About Makerspaces

Curious About Classroom Makerspaces? Here's How to Get Started by
   Angela Watson
https://thecornerstoneforteachers.com/makerspaces

Little Bins for Little Hands
https://littlebinsforlittlehands.com

Makerspaces in School by Lacy Brejcha
http://makerspacesinschool.com

Mrs. Brejcha's Class Website
https://sites.google.com/a/bosquevilleisd.org/mrs-brejcha-s-class

Makerspace, Enrichment & Innovation by Lacy Brejcha
https://goo.gl/photos/f9fZiMukiieEaioh7
   (*Note.* This site includes photos and videos available online via my
class webpage.)

Makerspace for Education
http://www.makerspaceforeducation.com

Renovated Learning: Makerspace Resources
http://renovatedlearning.com/makerspace-resources

Teachers Pay Teachers
https://www.teacherspayteachers.com
   (*Note.* Search "Makerspace," and pick a grade level to filter the
results.)

Social Media

Pinterest
Search for "STEAM Lessons," "Makerspace Ideas," "Makerspace Challenge Cards," "Makerspace Task Cards," etc.

Twitter
Browse hashtags, such as: #makerspace #makerspaces #steammakers #makered #makerspacesinschool

Coding Resources

Hour of Code
https://hourofcode.com/us

Hello World!: Computer Programming for Kids and Other Beginners by Warren and Carter Sande

Make Your Own Web Page—for Kids! by Ted Pederson and Francis Moss

Python for Kids: A Playful Introduction to Programming by Jason R. Briggs

Code Your Own series by Max Wainewright

About the Author

Lacy Brejcha has been an elementary education teacher for more than 15 years. She graduated from Baylor University in 2002. Currently, she is the GT district coordinator, elementary GT teacher, Makerspace teacher (innovation and enrichment), and instructional technologist at Bosqueville ISD. Her first book is *Makerspaces in School: A Month-by-Month Schoolwide Model for Building Meaningful Makerspaces.* Lacy has been married to Jim for 15 years, and they have two daughters—Brooke, who is 10 years old, and Grace, who is 6 years old. After building a successful Makerspace, she is excited to share how a Makerspace can work in your classroom, school, or district.